END OF THE

Enel Malakrist

Copyright 2020 by Enel Malakrist.

ISBN: 978-0-9884558-7-0

All rights reserved. No part of this book may be used or reproduced in any manner whatsoever without written permission, except in the case of brief quotations embodied in critical articles or reviews, and religious teaching. Please do not participate in or encourage the piracy of copyrighted materials in violation of the author's rights.

Unless otherwise indicated, the Bible quotations are taken from the King James Version of the Bible. Copyright 1945 by Oxford University Press, Inc.

TABLE OF CONTENTS

Chapter 1: Confirmed Covenant 1

Chapter 2: The Great Tribulation..8

Chapter 3: Two Witnesses 13

Chapter 4: The Antichrist..16

Chapter 5: Acts of the Antichrist..21

Chapter 6: The False Prophet..24

Chapter 7: Great Leader..29

Chapter 8: Vision of the Great Leader 33

Chapter 9: Primary Mission of the Great Leader..36

Chapter 10: Ancillary Mission of Great Leader 40

Chapter 11: Signs in the last days 46

Chapter 12: Pestilence 54

Chapter 13: End in Sight..60

Chapter 14: Rapture of the Redeemed 66

Chapter 15: Vision of the Rapture 70

Chapter 16: Conditions for Christ's appearing..72

Chapter 17: Caught Up 75

Chapter 18: Middle-East Conflict..78

Chapter 19: Invasion of Israel 81

Chapter 20: Battle for Jerusalem 83

Chapter 21: Antichrist Comes to Jerusalem 85

Chapter 22: World War-3 Unrelenting 88

Chapter 23: Angelic Pronouncements 90

Chapter 24: Investiture of the King 92

Chapter 25: Battle of Armageddon 94

Chapter 26: Coming Again 98

Chapter 27: Glorious Return 103

Chapter 28: A New World Order 107

References 110

CHAPTER 1

CONFIRMED COVENANT

The scriptures indicate that Daniel's prophetic treaty will be an agreement between the nation of the beast (Antichrist) and many nations. Recently, an international agreement of great significance has been reached between the leader of a nation of the Middle-East and many world leaders.

On July 14, 2015, after nearly two years of intense and arduous negotiations, the Islamic Republic of Iran and the permanent members of the United Nations, namely the United States of America, United Kingdom, France, China, and Russia along with Germany (EU) agreed to a historic nuclear treaty. The two main features of the accord are that Iran would defer building a nuclear bomb for a period of ten years and the nations would end their economic sanctions against Iran.

The Iran treaty is the only international agreement on record that appears to match Daniel's end-time prophecy of the confirmed covenant. The nuclear treaty between Iran and the world has identical markers to Daniel's predicted covenant. Firstly, the prophecy identified one participant of the treaty as a nation that is hostile to Israel.

Today, even while the treaty was being negotiated, Iran, as a nation, expresses extreme hostility towards Israel. Secondly, the treaty is made between Iran – the hostile nation against Israel and many nations. Thirdly, the prophecy specifies a time factor for the duration of the treaty. This is clearly expressed in the current agreement. Daniel predicted a term of seven years for the agreement, whereas the current agreement states a term of ten years. However, a close study of Daniel's writing reveals that an angel added twenty-three hundred days to Daniel's predicted seven years.[1] This extends the last days to thirteen years, three months, and twenty days. Daniel pointed out that those seven years were assigned to bring closure for the Jews while the aggregate thirteen years will bring closure to the Gentile rule.

Treaty Negotiation

The historic nuclear treaty between Iran and the nations is regarded as one of the most significant treaties of all times and may be the key to unlock the secrets of the last days. Consider the timing of the treaty negotiations. The nations negotiated with Iran for seventeen months, which began in February 2014 before reaching a final agreement.

Iran and the world powers, namely the United States, United Kingdom, France, Russia, China, and the European Union endorsed the agreement on 14th July in the Jewish Sabbatical in 2015. Observe that the negotiations and signing took place within the parameters of the lunar tetrad from April 2014 to September 2015 during the Jewish Sabbatical year.

The negotiations with Iran during those two years of intriguing celestial signs were very difficult. The Iranians took a hardliner position and held their ground using stalling tactics. Then on March 20, 2015, the total solar eclipse was observed in Tehran, Europe, and Jerusalem, and darkness covered the land for a period of time. In God's economy, darkness indicates judgment.

Suddenly, the Iranians agreed to a framework for an agreement. The interim agreement was endorsed on April 2, just two days before the

Passover blood moon. The interim agreement at the time of the solar eclipse and blood moon, when Israel celebrated the New Year and Passover was not a coincidence. Those signs seem to indicate a divine involvement in the proceedings.

Ratification of the Final Agreement

The final agreement of the Joint Comprehensive Plan of Agreement was signed on the 14th of July 2015 by Iran and six world powers. Subsequently, the agreement was presented to the United States Congress for review. The review date expired on September 17th without any action by the United States Congress.

Consequently, the agreement proceeded as approved on July 14. The Iranian Government also approved the agreement. On the 8th of October, the United Nations Security Council unanimously adopted resolution 2231/2015 affirming the 14th July agreement on Iran's nuclear program. Later on, Iran confirmed the treaty on October 14.

Celestial Signs during Treaty Negotiations

The celestial signs in 2015, which is the year of the ratification of the treaty are worthy of special notification. There were six notably celestial events during the two-year period of the negotiations. They were as follows; a total solar eclipse on the Jewish calendar New Year that darkened Europe, North Africa, and Western Asia was observed and a double eclipse of the sun on the Day of Trumpets (Rosh Hannah) September 13, 2015.

The eclipse was viewed by NASA's Solar Dynamics Observatory in space. NASA reported that this rare and unusual event was the first-ever seen or recorded occurrence.[2]

There were also four blood moons on divinely appointed Jewish feast days, two of which occurred during the Sabbatical year 2015 was very intriguing.

Secondly, it is noteworthy that a blood moon appeared over Jerusalem on the day of the Feast of Tabernacles, five days after the Day of Atonement (Yom Kippur). The nature and appearance of the blood moon of

September 28, 2015, should not be ignored. The eclipse took place when the moon was at its closest point to the earth. At that exceptional closeness, the moon appeared to be very large with a remarkably bright red color. This rare and unusual appearance of the moon; and the vast area of the earth where it was visible seem to be a divine sign and an omen.

The scriptures make it plain that the purpose of the moon and the sun is not only to give light to the earth but also to give divine signals to the inhabitants of the earth. "Let them be for signs and seasons and for days, and years"[3]. Therefore, celestial signs are divinely placed and should not be ignored. That spectacular blood red supermoon was without a doubt a divine signal to the world that a great event was about to take place.

Super Blood Moon

The bright blood red supermoon of September 28, 2015, was divinely positioned so that it was visible to the world powers from the Eastern Pacific to Western Asia. People in western China, India, and Moscow, Russia observed the rare celestial sign. Washington DC, the Americas, Africa, the islands, all European capitals, and Jerusalem observed that most spectacular celestial event. This total lunar eclipse over Europe and Western Asia followed on the heels of a solar eclipse in March, which darkened the countries that negotiated the Iran Agreement.

Apparently, the celestial position of the total lunar and solar eclipses were not by accident or coincidence. This super blood moon, together with the total solar eclipse and the rare and unusual double solar eclipse, an omen, on divinely appointed days appear to be sending a blunt message to the world while identifying an event of great biblical significance – the fulfillment of Daniel's confirmed covenant. The darkened sun of the solar eclipses implies judgment, whereas the blood moon signifies a promise.

Warning to the Nations

On September 28, 2015, a message was coded in the celestial sign that traversed the heavens and displayed to the inhabitants of over 80% of the habitable landmass of the earth. The super blood moon displayed its blood red color to the people on earth from the Eastern Pacific to Asia; from the North Pole to the South Pole. The moon was observed from the Pacific Ocean to the Indian Ocean with a coverage of at least 80% of the habitable landmass.

The message to the world powers is like the message that was written without hands on the wall of King Belshazzar's palace fifteen centuries ago. *"God has numbered your kingdoms and finished it. Thou art weighed in the balances, and found wanting."* [4]

The global viewing of super blood moon which occurred on September 28, 2015, on the divinely appointed Feast of Tabernacles is a sign directed to the nations of the world. The super blood moon on September 28, 2015, was a sign that a significant event was about to take place. The blood moon occurred at the time of the confirmation of the Iran Nuclear Treaty, just as a blood moon appeared at the signing of the treaty a few months earlier.

The super blood moon on the day of the Feast of Tabernacles within the viewing range of 80% of the nations is a divine signal to the world. It is a sign that a great catastrophe is coming upon the earth and the inhabitants of earth could be at risk.

Deciphering the Prophecy

All three elements for a correct prophetic interpretation must come into play for a particular event. These events are; the prophecy, fulfilling event' and celestial signs. All these converged at the historic event of the Iran nuclear agreement. These blood moon signs of 2014 - 2015 appeared at the time of the divinely appointed Israeli feasts and during the final stages of the international treaty negotiations with Iran, which seems to be a coincidence. Likewise, a total solar eclipse took place within a few days of the blood moon in 2015.

The occurrence of these rare celestial events at a crucial time of the Iran negotiations appeared to be a supernaturally ordained move to garner a positive outcome. The scriptures tell us that God uses signs in the Sun and

Moon to accomplish His divine purpose. God said, "Let there be lights in the expanse of the heavens to separate day and night; and let them be for signs and tokens [of God's provident care]."[5]

Proof that the Iran Nuclear Treaty Daniel's Confirmed Covenant

The Joint Comprehensive Plan of Action agreement is a historic agreement. This landmark agreement satisfies all the criteria of Daniel's prophecy of the treaty in the last days between the Prince from a far country and many nations.

The prophet also gave litmus tests to authenticate the fulfillment of the prophecy. Daniel wrote that the treaty will be between a prince and many other nations. The Iran deal was negotiated between Iran on one side and six countries on the other. Moreover, the treaty was eventually signed by Iran and over ninety other countries in the United Nations. This criterion was fully satisfied.

Secondly, the treaty lasted for seven years. However, it was finalized for ten years. This is not a great discrepancy. It came very close to the twenty-five-hundred-year-old prophecy of seven years. That criterion was also satisfied.

Thirdly, Daniel predicted that the treaty will be violated at midpoint. This prediction was fulfilled on May 8, 2018, three years after the signing of the deal. This is well within the limits of the midpoint of Daniel's expressed time frame. At that time, the United States, an original negotiator and signatory of the deal withdrew from the contract. The President then reimpose sanctions on Iran, thereby violating the terms of the agreement.

The supernatural input of dramatic signs during the final stages of the international negotiations, along with the verifying terms, leads a wise, spiritual-minded person to believe that the treaty is of divine significance. After reviewing all the evidence, it is concluded without a doubt that the Iran Nuclear treaty is the fulfilment of Daniel's predicted treaty (Confirmed Covenant) of the last days.

Accordingly, the ratification date of the treaty on July 14 2015, marks the first day of the tribulation and also the first day of the last thirteen years of the Common Era. The count down to the end has begun.

CHAPTER 2

THE GREAT TRIBULATION

The world is in a state of deteriorating moral and spiritual condition. Quite evidently, the nations are in the vise grip of an unprecedented spate of violence and immorality. Every moral law of God is being challenged and violated at all levels of society.

A civilized man has taken a giant step backward into the dark ages of ungodliness. The wickedness of man is great in the earth. Notably, the same type of declension that preceded Noah's flood is pervading the nations today. Just as it was in the days of Noah, so it is in this generation.

A world-changing event is about to take place. Brace yourself for the darkest days in human history. A devastating calamity is forthcoming. Millions could perish in the next ten years. The signs of the times, as foretold by the prophets, point to a coming world catastrophe.

Great disasters and severe distress will strike the nations during the next ten years. The unprecedented events will unfold as the days go by. Unfortunately, the coming world disasters will appear suddenly upon an unprepared generation.

The scriptures declare that *"there shall be a time of trouble [anguish and suffering]; such as never was since there was a nation [on the face of the earth] even to that same [future] time"*.[6] According to the scriptures, the world cannot escape the coming distress and oppression. Such fate is decreed upon the world in the last days. And the word of God must be fulfilled in its due season.

Jesus' dire prediction of great tribulation is presently being fulfilled in this generation. These are the last days as exposed by the fulfillment of Daniel's seventieth-week prophecy. The great tribulation is a time of unexampled manifestation of evil predicted to come upon the world. Jesus revealed that the tribulation will be *"The hour of temptation, which shall come upon all the world, to try (test) them that dwell upon earth"*.[7]

The afflictions and distress of the tribulation on humanity will be so severe that Jesus said if it lasts for the full predetermined time humanity would perish from the face of the earth. However, God in His mercy will cut the tribulation period short for the sake of the elect - His chosen ones.[8]

Time of the Great Tribulation

The beginning of the period of great distress is prophetically fixed to start on the day when the Antichrist enters Jerusalem and profane the holy sanctuary, and puts an end to the daily sacrifice. The angel told Daniel that the period is scheduled to continue for 2,300 days (6 years and 4 months 19 days).[9]

Jesus also gave a preview of the time of the great tribulation. He told His followers that the distress and unbearable anguish will begin at the time of the appalling sacrilege, which was prophesied by Daniel.[10]

The Antichrist is the one who will defile the sanctuary. The tribulation will therefore start when he enters Jerusalem and magnifies himself, and presumptuously enters the Temple, and compares himself to God. The date of the travesty is still unknown. However, it will be in the not too distant future, when the third Temple in Jerusalem is dedicated.

The great tribulation will be a time of divine chastisement for the nation of Israel because they rejected their Covenant with Jehovah; and it will also be a time of testing for all people on Earth.

The great tribulation is ordered by God to sift the church and the Jews, and to purge them of the unfaithful adherents. The tribulation will cause the separation of the wheat from the tares, and purify the church, and make her ready for the meeting of Christ in the sky.[11]

The prophet Daniel wrote that in the last days the transgressions of the Jews will reach their fullness, and come to a point that exceeds God's mercy. At that time, a king will arise and hold sway over Israel, and subjugate the Jews.[12] This king will be the Antichrist who will occupy Jerusalem. He will inflict the Jews for forty-two months.

The greatest transgression of Israel is 2,000 years of willful spiritual darkness, as a result of their determined rejection of Jesus Christ their Messiah. At the trial before Pilate on Wednesday morning, March 22, 23AD the Roman Judge found no fault with Jesus that was worthy of death; and he suggested that Jesus should be released. The Jews rejected Jesus and shouted *"Away with this man ... Crucify Him."*[13] The Jews rejected both Jesus and His teachings; and they have not obeyed the gospel. Again, the prophet declared that "Israel obeyed not the voice; she received not correction; she trusted not in the Lord; she drew not near to God."[14]

The prophet Jeremiah referred to the great tribulation as a sound of terror and of dread with no peace, and a time of Jacob's troubles.[15] The purpose of that punishment is to bring backsliding Israel back to her knees, and to bring them back to God at the time of the end before the coming of the Messiah.

The tribulation will also be a test for all people on earth. The church will not escape the misery of the last days. The awful period will come upon believers to test their faith, and prove their allegiance to God.[16]

The scriptures taught that all people on Earth, both rich and poor will be given the mark of the beast - 666. That mark signifies an act of allegiance to the Antichrist. Moreover, it will be a mark of Antichrist ownership. The mark will be impressed on the right hand, or on the forehead.

The mark will be voluntary. People will have a choice of taking the mark or refusing it. However, only people with the mark of the beast will be permitted to buy or sell or invest or receive banking services, or medical and social services.

All those who accept the mark of allegiance to the Antichrist and the Devil will be doomed on the Day of Judgment. People will be forced to worship the image of the beast, and those who refuse to bow will be killed.[17]

There will be severe restrictions in the near future. No one will be able to buy consumer goods, or transact any legal commercial transaction unless he displays the mark of the beast on his body.

Major wars have been predicted to break out during the tribulation period. Soon, the world will be plunged into another world war, and weapons of mass destruction will be deployed. The Bible revealed that the Fourth Seal, and the Fifth Trumpet are judgments of war.

Great distress will come upon the people of the Earth as a consequence of the global wars. The scriptures revealed that the death toll will be great. The Bible estimates that a quarter of the inhabitants will die from war related injuries, pestilence, and famine. The present world population is about seven and a half billion people. Therefore, the death toll will be as high as one billion.

Daniel's prophecy of the 70th week is specifically for the Jews. However, the impact of the reign of terror of the Antichrist (Prince of fierce countenance) will be felt by every nation on the surface of the Earth.[18]

The great tribulation will be the darkest days in human history. The world will be terrorized by the evilest despotic ruler to live on planet Earth. God will intervene in the affairs of man to prevent the nations from destroying the Earth and humanity. The afflictions of the tribulation will be so great that God will not permit it to run its full course. Global wars and anarchy will engulf the nations. Nations will be poised to destroy each other with thousands of nuclear weapons in their possession.

The Lord knows the intent of the hearts of man, and the end before the beginning. The Almighty will intervene to prevent an irreversible global catastrophe. The Lord will gather the wicked nations, and challenge them in battle.

God will display His awesome power and destroy the ungodly, warring nations at the battle of Armageddon.

CHAPTER 3

TWO WITNESSES

Scriptures revealed that God will send two witnesses to prophesy in Jerusalem during the Great Tribulation.[19] Their ministry is ordained for three and a half years, and will take place during the time of desolation. This is indicated as the time during when the Antichrist enters Jerusalem and profanes the holy sanctuary. This will most likely take place at a time during or after Daniel's predicted seven-year period.

The two witnesses are vaguely revealed in scriptures. The prophet Malachi referenced Elijah as one being sent to Jerusalem before the day of the Lord.[20] Likewise, Jude mentions Enoch prophesy of the coming of the Lord.[21] Enoch is the son of Jared, a descendant of Seth, and the seventh generation from Adam,[22] and Elijah the Tishbite, and a prophet of ancient Israel.[23]

These two witnesses were nonetheless positively identified in the Gospel of Nicodemus. The writer recorded the words of the witnesses - "One of them answering and said, I am Enoch, who was translated by the word of God: and this man who is with me, is Elijah he Tishbite, who was translated in a fiery chariot. Here we have hitherto been, and have not tasted death, but are now about to return at the coming of antichrist, being armed with divine signs and miracles, to engage with him in battle, and to be slain by him at Jerusalem, and to be taken up alive again into the clouds, after three days and a half."[24]

Both men were servants of God during the time of the Old Testament. They were supernaturally translated and taken to paradise, and never tasted death.[25] They will come back to Earth during the time of the great tribulation when the Antichrist occupies Jerusalem. They will be dressed in sackcloth. This is a loose outer garment made from very coarse material, usually goat's hair. This material was used to make grain sacks, and not clothing. Sackcloth garment symbolizes squalor, degradation, mourning, and repentance.

The witnesses will be in Jerusalem during the time of the Antichrist occupation. The Jews will be under severe religious persecution, and subjected to extreme hardship and suffering. The mission of God's two witnesses will be to preach to the Jews about the true and living God. Their preaching will cause a great spiritual awakening in Israel.[26] And the Jews will remember their God, and multitudes will call upon the name of the Lord.

The two witnesses will be endowed with supernatural powers, and will perform great miracles. They will have power to prevent rain from falling during the entire period of their ministry, and turn water into blood. They will also have power to strike the Earth with all manner of plagues as often as they desire.

Consequently, they will be hated by the occupying forces. If any man attempts to hurt them, they will spew fire from their mouths and kill them. No one will be able to apprehend them during the course of their ministry. However, they will be attacked and killed at the end of their predetermined forty-two months ministry. People will be scared to touch their corpses. Subsequently, their dead bodies will remain in the streets of Jerusalem for three and a half days.

Suddenly, life will return into their bodies. They will get up off the ground, and stand on their feet. Then a voice from heaven will call to them, and they will be lifted up off the ground, and the cloud will receive them.

CHAPTER 4

THE ANTICHRIST

A leader will rise up in the last days, and command great power, and authority in the world. Scriptures refer to that powerful leader as the Little Horn, "Man of sin," the Lawless one, the Antichrist, and the Beast. The popular name, Antichrist, will be used more often than any other, in reference to the powerful ruler.

Scriptures recorded that the Antichrist will emerge from the fragments of a nation which once ruled the world. Daniel unveils him as the Little Horn. This man will be ruler of the most powerful nation in the last days. The Antichrist will be a vile person, and a man without honor. He will be void of royalty, and majesty. He will be a contemptuous and despicable individual who is not worthy to be king. However, he shall become ruler by flatteries, intrigues, and cunning hypocritical conduct.

The Antichrist will become a powerful ruler. He will do according to his will, and will reject all counsel; and no one will dare to challenge him. He will be a great communicator and negotiator, but will not keep his word. He will make an alliance with others, and thereafter act deceitfully.

The Antichrist will have no respect for women. He will regard military power, and economic superiority. He will corrupt the nations, and cause astounding devastation, and will do as he pleases. He will think that he is superior to man, and will exalt and magnify himself above every god. He will speak evil things against the Most High God, and all those angels that dwell in heaven.

The Bible exposed him as a powerful ruler who will be boastful, and full of pride. He will hate the people of God, and seek to destroy the Jewish nation. During his reign when he feels secured, he will regard himself above all men. The Antichrist will exalt himself above everything that is godly. He will even proclaim himself to be God, and demand that everyone worships him.[27]

Appearing of the Antichrist

The Antichrist will be manifested in the last days when the apostate Jews has reached the point of transgression exceeding the limits of God's mercy.[28] Current history and the signs of the time strongly indicates that many Jews have lost interest in their religion, and have rejected their Covenant with Jehovah.

The Jewish people also overwhelmingly rejected the New Covenant, and the Gospel of salvation through Jesus Christ. The percentage of those who have rejected Jesus today is staggering. They overwhelmingly rejected Jesus two thousand years ago, and time has not changed their position. This very moment in time, in these last days about 99% of the Jewish people still reject Jesus Christ, and His teachings of the good news of salvation through faith.

Today, only a small minority of Jews in Israel numbering about one hundred thousand believes in Jesus Christ as Messiah. This marginal sect of believers calls themselves Messianic Jews believes. This group strictly adheres to their Jewish heritage, but accepts the New Covenant of salvation by faith through the blood of Jesus Christ; rather than atonement through the blood of bulls, and sheep under the law of the Old Covenant.

The scriptures give a definite order of events that will lead up to the time of the Antichrist. The first event relates to the church. There will be an apostasy of the professed church. Large numbers of Christian believers will fall away from the truth of the gospel, and follow after false doctrines. Also, many will crave after the lust of the world, and be drawn into the lust and pleasure thereof.

Secondly, the Spirit that restrains iniquity will be taken from the world and returned to heaven. The exit of the restrainer of evil makes way for the mystery of lawlessness to be revealed. The mystery of lawlessness is the hidden principle of rebellion against constituted authority.

At no time in history has rebellion against authority be compared to this generation. Lawlessness is a world-wide problem of epidemic proportion, and no country is spared. The degree of violent crimes, assaults, murders at the family level, in communities and at national levels are unprecedented. Moreover, terrorist organizations are destabilizing many nations, and creating constitutional havoc in many parts of the world.

The dragon (Satan) will give his power, his throne and dominion [the world] to the Antichrist, and as a result he will become very powerful[29]. In the original creation, God made Lucifer ruler of earth. He rebelled against God, and God destroyed Earth with the great pre-Adam floods. Then, the Earth became inhabitable. Lucifer's dominion was swept from under him, and he lost all authority over Earth; and with the loss of the dominion came a change in his name. He no longer is Lucifer, but now called Satan and the devil.

However, God renewed the Earth, and gave dominion of the renewed Earth to His new creature Adam. Satan returned to Earth and tricked Adam into breaking God's law. Adam fell from grace and thereby lost the dominion. Satan then claimed the dominion once more, but this time as a pseudo ruler.

The scriptures point to Satan's claim of ownership of the world at the time of the temptation of Jesus by the devil/Satan. At that time, he promised to give all the kingdoms of the world to Jesus if He pays homage to him, and worship him. Jesus promptly rebuked the devil, and told him that he should worship God, and serve Him only.[30]

Identifying the Antichrist

Satan the adversary, never gives up. He just keeps on pushing, and devising new strategies to deceive God's people. He always seeks to use man to rebel against God. Satan knew that his end was near, and desired to make another bold move against God and His creatures.

Satan reached in his old playbook, and decided to appeal to man's instinct and weakness. He will target man's basic instincts of greed and pride, and entice him with an offer which he will not be able to refuse. In these last days, Satan will make the same offer of world domination to the antichrist. Then, antichrist will gladly accept Satan's offer.

Satan will then infuse his demonic powers into the antichrist; and give him his throne, and great dominion, and authority. The antichrist will be an egocentric person. He will exalt himself above human beings, and above God, regard himself as a superior genius.

The coming of the antichrist will be through the activity, and working of Satan in the world. The antichrist will have great influence over the nations. He will have unlimited affinity to evil and wickedness. He will perform many false miracles and wonders. He will seduce many godly believers by his policies, wicked deceptions, and lead them astray.

Many Christian and Jewish believers will fall away from the truth, and gravitate towards the Antichrist. Consequently, God will send a strong delusion to make those professing, fake Christians, and apostates believe lies.[31]

Those false believers will continue to worship God with their lips, but their hearts are far from God. They are people who resist the truth, and remain unconvinced by facts. They will ignore truth, and follow after the unrighteous, lawless, and lying Antichrist.

The apostle Paul wrote that a period of lawlessness will precede the Antichrist. Paul referred to him as the man of sin, and the lawless one.

The lawless one will disregard all constitutional laws and norms. He will even set convicted criminals free. He will encourage his servants and associates to break the law with impunity. The lawless one will be the author of lies, and will put truth to the ground.[32]

CHAPTER 5

ACTS OF THE ANTICHRIST

The Antichrist will extend his authority beyond the borders of his empire. To a greater or lesser degree, his policies will impact on every nation for a period of forty-two months[33]. At a certain point in his reign, he will become the devil's servant, and persecute the church, and the Jews. The persecution of the worshippers of the true God is in accordance with the plans of the devil, to turn people from God.

John the revelator wrote: *"And it was given unto him to make war with the saints, and to overcome them: and power was given him over all kindred, and tongues, and nations. And all that dwell upon the earth shall worship him, whose names are not written in the book of life of the Lamb slain from the foundation of the world. If any man has ears to hear, let him hear."*[34]

The Antichrist will build his armies, and with superior weapons in his arsenal, he will gain military superiority over many nations. Having superior armaments, he will flex his military muscles, and enforce his will on other nations. The antichrist will be ruthless and many nations will fear him. In the later days of his reign, he will declare himself as the undisputed ruler of the world.

The Antichrist is depicted as the little horn in the prophecy of Daniel. He will pretend to be a friend of Israel, and an ally. In the last days, the Antichrist will enter Jerusalem. He will magnify and portray himself as savior of the Jews.

Many people with wisdom and understanding, and insight will recognize the evil intent and deceitfulness of the Antichrist. They will resist the wicked dictator, but will be persecuted and silenced.

However, many Jews will lose courage, and desert their moral principles and faith, and approve of him wholeheartedly. The nation of Israel will honor the Antichrist for his great achievements as world leader.

The Antichrist will be puffed up with pride, and magnify himself as a god. He will demand that the daily sacrifice to God be halted. He will erect a statue of himself on Temple Mount, and compel the Jews to worship the statue under penalty of death.

The Antichrist will sit in the holy sanctuary on Temple Mount, and proclaim himself to be God and demand homage from all men.[35] Thereby, all those whose names are not written in the Lamb's Book of Life will fall down and worship him.[36]

As a consequence of the transgressions of the Jews: their irreverence, lack of devoutness and ungodliness, God will give them over to the antichrist. The Antichrist will occupy Jerusalem, and will exercise power and authority over Israel for three and a half years. The Antichrist's rule in Jerusalem will start at the end of Daniel's seven-year period; possible dating from the year 2022.[37]

Truth will be suppressed, and righteousness will be cast to the ground. Worship of God will cease, and the sanctuary will be profaned.[38] The Antichrist will have full authority over Jerusalem, and will oppress and persecutes the Jews and Christians; and all people who refuse to pay him homage.[39] Nonetheless, many Jews will submit to the Antichrist, and worship his image, and give him all the honor and praise.

The Antichrist will have no regard for the people of God, or for anyone. He will cause intolerable conditions to bear on the Jews, and on Christians, and upon all people within his nation and beyond. Anguish, misery and despair are decreed, and there will be war until the end. This will fulfill the scriptures that the Gentiles will trample the holy city of Jerusalem under foot[40]. The days of the Antichrist's rule will be the darkest and most ungodly period in the history of the world.

The Apostle John prophesied that the Antichrist will suffer a life-threatening malady. His condition will be critical. The prophet referred to his injury as a deadly wound – an injury from which he would not be expected to recover. However, he will miraculously recover, and completely healed of his injuries. John wrote that *"I saw one of his heads as it were wounded to death: and his deadly wound was healed, and all the world wondered after the beast."*[41]

The Antichrist will continue his ruthless reign over the nations. He will come to an end during the Battle of Armageddon. The Lord's troops will capture him, and his reign will end suddenly. The Lord will find him guilty of serious misdeeds, and he will be thrown into the Lake of Fire.

CHAPTER 6

THE FALSE PROPHET

The false prophet will be the second beast described by John in the book of Revelation. John wrote that a second beast will appear out of the earth. He will have the appearance of a lamb, but he will roar like a dragon. This beast ranks a little lower in status to the first beast [Antichrist]. He will be in subordination to the Antichrist, and a loyal servant. He will be the right-hand man of the Antichrist: And a shrewd twister of laws to accommodate the ideas and plans of the Antichrist.

The false prophet will enforce all the wishes, and decrees of the Antichrist. He will enforce a religion of cult worship, and idolatry upon the world; and decree that all people must worship the Antichrist. As a display of commission and superiority, he will perform startling miracles in the presence of the Antichrist.

The false prophet will be a master magician. He will seek to perform seemingly impossible tricks. He will even display fire coming down from high in the sky in full view of people. All those miraculous powers will be given to him by the supernatural. However, he will not be able to practice the supernatural powers on his own. He will be able to perform only in the presence of the Antichrist. By amazing signs and wonders, the Antichrist right-hand man will deceive the people, and give the impression that the Antichrist who survived the deadly injuries is deity.

The false prophet will command that a statue in the likeness of the Antichrist be erected in his honor in Jerusalem. A supernatural power will permit the false prophet to give life to the statue. The statue will then speak and command all those who refuse to bow down, and worship the image to be killed.[42]

The idea of a statue speaking is not far-fetched. The technology is here today. Advancement in robotic technology has made it possible to create lifelike copies of humans. These human robots called androids are sophisticated electronic masterpieces encased in plastic.

By the use of a computer and a microphone, the operator can capture the voice of the individual being imitated. At the same time, the computer can track both face, head and arm movements. It can even capture blinks, twitches and the appearance of breathing, which is replicated by the android.

Some androids are programmed to answer questions, and give directions. Anyone who uses the telephone to call a major corporation will talk to an android (robot) with a human voice. Likewise, any driver who uses the GPS system will be given driving directions by an android (robot) with a human voice. Androids can be programmed to hold conversations, and give instructions in the voice of any human being.

The assistant to the antichrist will also function as a secretary of trade and commerce, and enforcer of laws. He will decree that everyone receives a mark on the forehead or on the right hand. The mark will bear the name of the beast [Antichrist], or the number of his name which is 666. That imprint will be a mark of allegiance to the Antichrist. Loyal individuals with the mark will be allowed to buy or sell goods and receive services. The mark of the beast will be voluntary. However, all people without the mark will be denied the right to buy, sell, and receive services.

The imprint on the forehead and right hand may not be a literal name or the number 666. The technology of these last days are so advanced that a more discreet mark will be used instead of words or numerals. A synonym for mark is chip. A chip is a small piece of something. In the world of technology, a chip is a small piece of silicon with an electronic circuit embedded into it. Human chips are very small capsules about the size of a grain of rice.

Today, microchips for human implants are approved by the United States Food and Drug administration (FDA). Chips can be coded with many personal information such as identity, social security number, health history, credit card, and banking. Micro chipping is also the perfect method to engrave the mark of the beast-666 on people. The information on the chip can be retrieved by scanning with a computer device.

Microchip implants are currently being tested on individual volunteers. Notably, the choice place on the body where the chip is implanted is under the skin, at the back of the hand; between the thumb and the first finger. Incidentally, the Bible recorded that the number 666 (mark of the beast) will be on the right hand. The prophecy was spoken 2,000 years ago, and it is right on target. These are the last days, and without a doubt, the mark of the beast is in the very near future.

The mark of the beast will test the loyalty, and faithfulness of Christian believers, and Jews, and all people on Earth during the period of severe austerity, hardship, and persecution under the Antichrist[43]. Insincere and weak believers will lose courage during the difficult days, and desert their faith in God. Therefore, the mark of the beast will serve to purge the church of fake believers.

The Lord will use the test to refine, and purify the church and get her ready for the coming of Christ: like the five wise virgins whose lamps were trimmed, and were prepared, and ready to meet the Bridegroom at the midnight cry.

The mark of the beast will be no surprise to God. It is predicted in scripture according to God's plan and purpose for the people in the last days. Like a grade school test, the mark of the beast test determines who moves up to glory, and who is left behind.

Any believer who accepts the mark either by economic pressure, or for want of the basic elements of survival, or coercion, or threat by the Antichrist, openly testifies that he becomes loyal to the beast. Such a believer publicly denounces his faith, and has become an apostate Christian or Jew, will be accursed and damned on the Day of Judgment, and tormented with fire and brimstone. (Revelation 14:10)

The church in the last days will not escape the horrors of the tribulation. Bible prophecy reveals that the saints will suffer persecution in the last days[44]. Believers living in the days of the great tribulation under the reign of the Antichrist must be prepared to die for their faith in Jesus Christ, and the gospel. They must be ready to endure severe hardship and oppression by the evil rulers. They will get hungry and thirsty, but must not sell their soul for bread or water. Bear in mind that you are under a test, and God do not abandon you. Jesus will be watching over you and will grade your performance under stress and persecution.

The believer must not give up or give in to the tormentors. Remember that Jesus suffered the cruelest, and unusual punishment of death on the cross to save mankind from eternal death. It is fitting then that those who receive salvation should also take up their cross, and suffer for their faith during the time of a divinely ordered test.

All people will face death, and it is better for the believer to die for his faith in Jesus Christ, than to take the mark of the beast and die as a follower of the antichrist, and enter into eternal damnation. Only those believers who endure the attacks of the enemy, and get the victory will be counted worthy to reign with Christ when He comes. Therefore, the prize of a crown of the righteous at the end of the test will be worth more than the suffering.

Remember the promises of Jesus. He said *"He that overcometh shall inherit all things;"* and the righteous will be with Him in His Father's kingdom. All backsliders, apostates, and those who receive the mark of the beast will be doomed on the Day of Judgment. They will not enter into the kingdom of heaven, or have any part or lot with Jesus Christ.

CHAPTER 7

GREAT LEADER

A leader will rise up from among one of the nations that was once part of the Roman Empire. He will grasp great power and exercise authority over many nations. The prophet Daniel describes that individual as a future prince and a powerful ruler, emerging from a nation which once ruled the world.[45] The Great Leader will be a powerful ruler. He will elevate and magnify himself above everyone, am every god: and will say unheard-of things against the God of heaven.

Leaders are not born great. Greatness is a characteristic of the individual. They achieve greatness due to circumstances which they face and boosted by their ego. Even so, it is God who promotes men to greatness. The scriptures declared that "The Most High God rules in the kingdom of men, and that He appoints and sets over it whomsoever He wills."[46]

Therefore, anyone in the hand of God can become great by serving His divine purpose. Consequently, God not only calls leaders, but He equips them for specific purposes.

These rulers unknowingly are made great to do the will of God, and fulfill His divine promises. The scriptures plainly stated that the king's heart is like channels of water in the hand of the Lord, and he turns it wherever he wishes.[47] A good Biblical example is Cyrus, king of Persia. Cyrus was born 600 BC, six years after the first deportation of Jews to Babylon. The Lord called Cyrus by name, one hundred years before he was born.[48]

God gave King Cyrus great power to conquer nations and build the great Persian Empire. Then, in the year 586 BC, the Jews had completed seventy years captivity in Babylon, fulfilling Jeremiah's prophecy.[49] The time came for the Jews to return to their homeland according to Jeremiah's prophecy.

God always performs the counsels of his messengers and fulfills their prophecies. At that time, God stirred the mind of Cyrus to release the Jews from Babylonian captivity, and decree the building of the walls of Jerusalem, and rebuild the Temple which was destroyed by the Babylonians.

In the year 536 BC, Cyrus the idol-worshiping heathen king unknowingly fulfilled the purpose of his divine calling. God hereby shows that all creation is at His beckoning, and He can use anyone irrespective of spirituality, morality or character to serve His divine purpose. Note that God did not seek to convert the heathen king, but used him in his current spiritual state.

The fact that Cyrus fulfilled God's purpose is not any indication that God approved of his heathen lifestyle. Jesus plainly stated that some men will do great works in the name of the Lord; they will preach, prophesy, heal the sick, cast out devils, and many wonderful works in Jesus name, yet if their heart is not right with God they will not enter into eternal life.[50] The scriptures declared that God disapproves of every form of ungodliness, and will not acquit the sinner.[51]

Artaxerxes, king of Persia and grandson of Cyrus the Great was also moved by God to show favor to the Jews. In 444 BC, he decreed that the Jews return to Judah, and build the walls of Jerusalem, fulfilling Daniel's prophecy.[52] There are prophecies to be fulfilled in these last days, and God is still calling men to fulfill His divine words.

God is still calling men in this generation, and preparing them, and making them great, and appointing them to fulfill His divine purpose in these last days. As it was in the past, God can use anything and anyone to fulfill His divine purpose. He can use religious people, and He can use men of ill-reputation. All men and all things are at God's disposal to do His will. The scriptures revealed that God used a donkey to reprimand one of His prophets.

The Lord is sovereign ruler of planet Earth, and all things are done according to His divine purpose and plan.[53] God can and will use a man to fulfill His divine purpose in these last days. However, one should recognize that God's plans are not always in line with the plans of man. A man may be called, and empowered to build up in one location, and to destroy in another.

In these last days, God will call a man who though despised by many; the Lord will place him in the seat of authority, as ruler of the nation. Such a man will be equipped by God, and given an unwavering mind-set to accomplish things that God will place in his mind.

The great leader will be the ruler of the world's most powerful nation. He will be very imposing, and will exercise great authority over the nations of the world. He will have a skeptical nature, and slow to trust others.

The great leader will surround himself with knowledgeable advisors, but will cast their counsel aside, and instead rely on his intuition, and act according to his thoughts. The great leader will go where no one dares. He will do the seemingly impossible things with surprising results. He is a master of craft, and a great negotiator who will only settle on his terms. A man who accepts no fault, and is quick to play the blame game, and will apologize to no one.

All the characteristics of the Little Horn (Antichrist) will be embodied in the great leader. He will seek to set aside all laws, and norms that hinders his plans, or stampedes his progress. He will demand total loyalty from all his servants. He will be very vindictive, and execute punishments on all those who oppose him, and reward those who praise him, and pay homage to him.

The great leader will think of himself as a genius who knows all things. He will never admit faults, and will apologize to no one. He will have little or no regards or respect for women. But he will honor the great leaders and dictators. He will be puffed up with pride and magnify himself above all men.

The prophet Daniel wrote that the great leader will be a powerful king, who will rule a kingdom made up of descendants from people of the ancient Roman Empire. John the revelator described him as the ruler of the beast (nation) that arose from the sea of men.

The nation of reference by Daniel and John, points to the United States of America. This is the only nation in the world whose citizenry is entirely made up of immigrants, drawn from all the former countries of the old Roman Empire.

Assuredly, these are the last days. Without any controversy, the United States is the most powerful nation on Earth today. One can dare to say with pride, and confidence that the United States is the most powerful nation ever to rule on Earth, and the great leader in these last days is the president.

CHAPTER 8

VISION OF THE GREAT LEADER

In a vision on June 27, 2003, I found myself all alone in a large enclosed room, right on the upper floor of a building. The room was sealed shut. There were no doors, no windows, no furniture, no light fixtures in the room, yet the room was well illuminated. Suddenly, and mysteriously, a very handsome young man dressed in a long flowing white robe appeared at the far side of the room.

The stranger's sudden appearance out of thin air startled me. Immediately, I froze as I was so scared. He had the appearance of an angel. How did he come into the room with no entryway? He looked at me and smiled reassuringly. I interpreted the friendly smile to mean that he did not come as an adversary. He calmly greeted me and all fear was gone. He never moved from the far corner. Then, he told me that he is from a far country and had come to a university in Virginia, from where he will learn about the customs and lifestyle of the people.

He then said to me, *"The Great Leader is here"*. He further informed me that the leader will oppress, persecute people, and will cause many to be killed. I took my eyes off him for a second and he was gone. He left as suddenly and as quietly as he came. I woke up from my sleep and wrote an account of the vision. I pondered on the dream for quite a while.

Without a doubt, the Great Leader revealed in the dream is one who rules during the time of Daniel's fulfilled prophecy of the confirmed covenant. All indicators for the time of the fulfillment of that prophecy points to July 14, 2015.

The angel did not reveal the name of the Great Leader in the dream of June 27, 2003. However, thirteen years later, a remarkable clue showed up in the sky for all to see. Lo and behold, a surreal image of Donald Trump's profile suddenly appeared in a cloud formation. This occurred in August 2016, over Black Canyon City, in the state of Arizona in United States of America.

The photograph of the image in the cloud was taken by Kent Reylek, who was in the right place at the right time with his camera. The image was broadcast by newsfeed and picked up by newspapers, TV stations, and social media all over the country. The miracle image prompted many Trump supporters to say that his profile in the sky is an indication that God chose him for the next president.

What's so intriguing about this is that Donald Trump was the underdog candidate in the election for president of the United States. It is noteworthy that Donald Trump was down in the polls at that time with no chance of winning the presidential election. This scenario is amazing! This is a sure confirmation that Donald Trump is the Great Leader of which the angel informed me in a dream.

Trump lost out on the popular vote in the presidential election on Tuesday, November 8, 2016. However, he gained the majority of the Electoral College votes on December 19, 2016. According to the constitution, the electoral college votes decide the winner of the presidential election. Donald Trump was then declared president-elect by the electoral college.

Consequently, Trump was installed the 45th president of the United States on January 17, 2017; 23 weeks after the image appeared in the sky over the state of Arizona. Considering the unexpected turn of the campaign events in which Trump was so far back in the polls, to win was nothing short of a miracle. This is suggestive of a supernatural influence in the election. Therefore, it is reasonable to conclude that the image in the sky, formed by the clouds, was a way to identify the Great Leader of the vision.

Trump in the clouds:

Photo: Credit Kent Reylek. He took the photo over Black

Canyon City Arizona, in 2016, during the presidential campaign.

The photo show clouds formed the profile image of Donald Trump.

CHAPTER 9

PRIMARY MISSION OF THE GREAT LEADER

God calls men and makes them great to fulfill His plans. The Lord calls men and promotes them to be rulers over nations.[54] God then uses them as instruments in His hand to fulfill prophecy, or to discipline, and chastise other nations in accordance with His divine plan.

All men belong to God, whether they are righteous or wicked; and He uses whomsoever He chooses. God called King Nebuchadnezzar his servant although he was a heathen and an idol worshipper. Yet, the Lord used him to fulfill His divine plan.

The purpose of Nebuchadnezzar's calling was to invade Judah and take the Jews into captivity.[55] God also called King Cyrus His servant. Yet, Cyrus was a heathen king, and also a worshipper of idols. Cyrus' calling was to fulfill Jeremiah's prophecy that the Jews will be returned to Judah seventy years after they were taken captive by the Babylonians.[56]

The profile image of Donald Trump in the clouds was the revelation of the person referenced in the vision as the great leader. With that in mind, it is reasonable to conclude that Donald Trump was called and promoted to rule by the Divine appointment. It is also believed that he was called to fulfill God's purpose and plan for Israel in these last days, just as it was with King Nebuchadnezzar and King Cyrus centuries ago.

Trump is no saint. Like most people, he has spiritual flaws and moral failures like those ancient kings. However, his failures and shortcomings did not preclude him from the service of the Lord. God knows the heart of man, and He chooses people who are strong and bold and position them to do great things for Him.

The affirmed Great Leader as outlined hitherto before closely fits the profile of Donald Trump, President of the United States of America. He is a man of very strong character, with a degree of authoritarian tendency. President Trump is a powerful ruler. He is acclaimed as the most powerful man on earth today. He exhumes such confidence that he arrogantly ascribes greatness upon himself.

President Trump describes himself as a stable genius and a man with unmatched wisdom. He delights in praise, and adoration, and demands absolute loyalty. No mountain will stand in his way, and no one will prevent him from achieving his goal. President Trump makes decisions on a whim according to his will and pleasure.

President Trump is truly a leader as no other and none can compare to him. He is an altruist; a firm supporter of Israel and seems to assume the role of a guardian angel and protector of the Jewish state. Trump's heart is moved towards the state of Israel. With the nations against Israel, Trump may well be the leader with a divine assignment to ally with Israel to fulfill end time prophecies concerning the Jewish state.

These are the waning hours of the last days, all prophecies must be fulfilled before the end. The call of the president of the United States appears to be two-fold. Firstly, it was a call to stand firm and support Israel when the world hates the Jewish nation. The state of Israel was reestablished in 1948, thereby fulfilling Ezekiel's prophecies. Unfortunately, the nation of Israel is still under the strong restrictive policies of the gentiles. Israel is living in their land, but their destiny as a fully sovereign nation is hindered by many nations, who seek her demise.

The rulers of many nations disregard the scriptures and reject Bible records of Israel, and erroneously claim that Israel has no ties with Jerusalem. Those ungodly nations scheme together in an effort to deprive Israel of her capital city, Jerusalem, and the sacred temple site. The United Nations even passed resolutions denying Jewish connections to Jerusalem, and that the holy site of Temple Mount belongs to the Muslims.

Moreover, on November 5, 2019, one hundred and forty-eight nations ignorantly voted to reject the name Temple Mount, and reordered the name of the holy mountain with eleven nations voting for Israel. They voted to remove the name Temple Mount from United Nations records and replace it with the Muslim name, Haram al-Sharif.

Jerusalem is the center of conflict between the Jews and the Palestinian Arabs. Jerusalem and the holy sites were Israel's possessions for over three thousand years. Both Bible records and secular history proves that fact.

These are the last days and Jerusalem and the holy sites must be liberated before the coming of the Messiah. However, Israel is capable of liberating her treasured sites. However, the risk will be too great going alone. Israel needs a nation with great power on her side as an ally. A nation led by a powerful ruler to stand with her to neutralize the negative effects of taking control of her possessions.

The call of Donald Trump from the Israeli perspective is obvious by the favors granted to Israel in these last days. The calling is to fulfill prophecy and to prepare Israel for the time of the end. President Trump decreed on Israel's behalf just as the ancient Persian kings did for the Jews.

The Jews were deprived of their capital city for 1,890 years, and President Trump, without hesitation, decreed that Jerusalem is the capital of Israel.

He then affirmed his decree by moving the American embassy to the city. Soon thereafter, many other nations followed suit and recognized Jerusalem as the capital of Israel.

The president further decreed that the Golan Heights are Israel's territory, and Israel immediately annexed that land. Trump also proposed a peace treaty between Israel and the Palestinians. That treaty was weighted heavily against the Palestinians. It gave Israel large swaths of lands in the West Bank territories to Israel. It also gave Israel a secured eastern border.

Moreover, the time has come for the building of the Temple and the fulfillment of the prophecies of Isaiah and Micah. Isaiah predicted that "In the last days the mountain of the LORD'S Temple will be established as chief among the mountains; it will be raised above the hills, and all nations will stream to it".[57] The prophet saw the Temple in the last days as the Temple of the Lord and the international center of worship.

The Lord will move the heart of the Great Leader to stand firm with Israel in a time of trouble. A man who will defy the hateful, ungodly nations who plot to hold Jerusalem and the holy sites hostage will emerge. A man who will defy the world body, and proclaim that the entire city of Jerusalem to be Israel's sovereign territory, and should be free from all external interference.

This decree will liberate Temple Mount and clear the way for Israel to build their third Temple on its original site. This will fulfill the word of God at the mouths of the prophets Isaiah, and Micah, which declared that the temple will be built in the last days.[58]

Any leader who pulls off such an impossible exploit will no doubt, be honored and esteemed, and rewarded by Jews worldwide. Moreover, he will go down in history and be regarded by the Jews as the greatest world leader since Cyrus the Great, King of the ancient Persian Empire.

CHAPTER 10

ANCILLARY MISSION OF GREAT LEADER

There seems to be a mystery relating to the call of the great leader. There may be a secondary purpose for Donald Trump's assenting to the presidency of the United States. Whatever way this is perceived, calling Donald Trump to lead the greatest nation in the world is rather puzzling.

This man, with no governance experience, no statesmanship qualities, was never elected to anything. Donald Trump is regarded as an egocentric narcissist with authoritarian tendencies, yet he was chosen to rule over the world's greatest free democratic nation.

The call of such a man as Donald Trump to rule over America is truly mystifying. He closely mirrors the nature and character of the Little Horn of Daniel's prophecy. He is a man obsessed with power. He is a future ruler in the last days, described by Paul as a lawless man. A man who bends all laws, rules, and norms to get them to fit his plans. A ruler who casts truth down to the ground at will, as prophesied by Daniel.

It is believed that President Trump holds the record for the falsest statements by any world leader in recorded history. Recently, the Washington Post in an article on June 1st, 2020, stated that in his first 1,226 days in office, May 29, 2020, President Trump has made 19,127 false claims and statements, according to the Facts Checkers database. This averages a whopping 15.6 lies per day. Could President Trump be the Little Horn and the lawless one of Bible prophecy? No one knows. However, these are the last days of the Common Era and he could well be the great leader to close out the era.

Some may argue that God did not call Donald Trump to be ruler over America on account of his past comportment. Nevertheless, the thoughts and ways of man are different from the thoughts and ways of God.

God is sovereign and He does as He pleases in heaven and on earth. The Lord works according to His divine plan and purpose, and His ways are perfect. Moreover, the scriptures made it plain that God rules in heaven and on earth. He rules over the nations, and He places over them whomever He pleases and they will turn their thoughts to accomplish His divine purpose.

Without a doubt, America has fallen from grace and is prime for divine chastisement. The Lord knows the heart of all mankind, and President Trump may well be the one chosen; who through ignorance, will unintentionally bring America to her knees.

America was founded and rooted in the word of God and has become the greatest and most powerful nation on earth for the last 75 years. However, America has become arrogant and ungodly. The church has become cold, and the nation has sidelined God and has adopted humanistic principles.

National America has rejected the word of God. She cast aside God's Laws on sodomy and enshrined homosexual laws in their constitution. America seems to devalue human life. The country has enacted laws legalizing abortion and denying the sanctity of life. Violence has become a way of life and thousands of people are licentiously murdered every year.

Moreover, America promotes gay rights and a perverted lifestyle, and many ungodly trends to the world. America has become boastful, arrogant, and full of pride in her military and economical greatness.

The Bible declares that God resists the proud. This was the case of Belshazzar, the proud Babylonian King, who saw the writing on the wall that declared that the kingdom will be taken away from him. America is at that same ill-fated place today. The writing is not on the wall, but in the imagined body of a tweet saying "America is weighed in the balance and is found wanting." Of a truth, America comes up spiritually short, and God is watching.

Trump's proven lack of national leadership, his pride, and unwillingness to accept advice from his counsellors qualifies him for the task of chastising America.

Leadership failure invariably results in failure of the country. This nation is too powerful to be conquered by the enemy, but can of a certainty fall under poor presidential leadership.

Therefore, it is opinionated that Donald Trump is the great leader of the last days as portrayed in the vision. Undoubtedly, he is the designated fall guy to inflict punishment on America in this time of great tribulation for her misdeeds.

Moreover, he was divinely promoted to the presidency at this crucial time in history, to be the instrument that the Lord would use to support the Jewish state.

Today, the greatest country in the world is reeling from the worst pandemic of the century. President Trump who in January, 2020, dubbed himself the commander-in-chief of the battle against Covid-19, has failed to control the defiant pathogen. Partly because he ignored the science of the pandemic, and then misrepresented, and down-played the dangers of the disease.

The President grossly mismanaged the public health crisis. Consequently, over six million Americans contracted the severely debilitating disease, and over one hundred and eighty-five thousand died up to this point. The needless suffering and heartbreak of millions of families could have been avoided to a certain degree, with good national leadership. Therefore, the pandemic debacle can be regarded as presidential malpractice.

As a result of the devastating pandemic, the economy goes into a freefall, and is getting worse by the day. There are civil disturbances which are mixed into the equation, and there is no coherent strategy or unifying leadership, or any workable plan to extricate the country out of these terrible crises.

The Covid-19 pandemic, and the severe economic depression, are only the beginning of sorrows under Donald Trump. Even so, he may well assume a second term as ruler by way of a miracle or trick. Nonetheless, whatever the outcome of the election, America should prepare for a strong dose of fascism.

According to a recent television interview, President Trump remarked that he may not accept defeat in the upcoming presidential election. Should that be the case, there may be no peaceful transfer of power, for the first time in the two hundred- and forty-years history of the United State of America.

President Trump indicated that he may not accept a democratic outcome of the elections. Thereby, he is setting the stage for a constitutional crisis by casting doubt on a fair outcome of the November elections. He claims, without any proof, that the election will be rigged against him. He further claims that there will be election fraud by his opponents to prevent him from winning the election.

Notwithstanding the multiple crises facing his administration, President Trump with the help of foreign actors, could well be declared winner of the November Election. Trump will not leave any stone unturned. He is fixated on winning. He plans to use every tactic to win.

Should he not win, then he will use every ploy to stay in the White House. There will be an attempt to forcefully remove Trump from the White

House to preserve democracy. Such an attempt may infuriate his supporters, and without a doubt, lead to widespread civil unrest. One can predict that there will be mega demonstrations, and marches, and riots in many cities.

Eventually, armed conflict will ensue between Trump's supporters presenting paramilitary groups on one side, and anti-trump activists on the other. The police and the national guards will be fully activated. However, some may side with Trump, and the stage will be set for a devastating civil war.

The prospect of a civil war will not deter Trump from pursuing his diabolic plan of fascism. He will sacrifice millions of lives to achieve his goals. Over the past four years his actions prove to the nation that he has no regards for rules, laws or the constitution. According to one report, his sister remarked that Trump has no principles, and he should not be trusted. She should be taken seriously.

America will be changed forever if Trump prevail and assumes a second term as president. He will institute a form of fascism not seen since Hitler ruled Germany. A new order of dictatorial governance may replace America's centuries-old democracy. Undemocratic changes, mass persecution, subjugation, and a reign of tyranny will begin. No form of opposition will be tolerated. He will persecute all his perceived enemies. Even those who supported him, and then disagree with his new policies will be perceived as enemies of the state, and will punished. Rest assured that minorities and the church will not escape his wrath.

Upon the president's decree, the state will distribute all benefits, based on loyalty, and allegiance to the leader. Accordingly, state generated identification numbers could be given his supporters, and also to those that pay homage to him. Consequently, only people with the special identification number, or possess a designated bodily mark, will receive benefits from state-run businesses and services.

Donald Trump, the great leader will rule with power and authority, and all people in America must comply, and adhere to his policies. Undoubtedly, these will be the days of great tribulation.

CHAPTER 11

SIGNS IN THE LAST DAYS

Two thousand years ago, Jesus Christ, the son of God, walked upon this earth. He was domiciled in Israel and lived in the region of Galilee. He spent His final week in Jerusalem and visited the Temple every day with His disciples. He had many sermons in the inner court of the Temple daily, as worshippers came to hear His teachings.

On Monday evening, Nisan 12 (March 21st, 23 AD), after His dissertations, Jesus departed from the Temple the last time. His disciples were filled with pride and awe at the magnificence of the Temple buildings and the richness and beauty of the gifts which adorned the sanctuary. As the evangelical party walked through the huge columns and porticos, the disciples could not help but point out to Jesus the architectural grandness of the Temple and all the surrounding buildings. Jesus listened as He walked down the long series of steps leading from the Temple. The party proceeded on the road to the Mount of Olives.

As they walked slowly up the hill, Jesus predicted that the Temple will be completely demolished and not even a single stone will be seen on top of another. They finally reached their destination on the Mount of Olives overlooking Jerusalem. There they could see the Temple in the distance below.

Jesus chose a spot and sat down under an olive tree. Then the disciples then gathered around Him. With much interest, they asked Jesus to tell them the time when such a disaster will befall the Temple. They also asked Him for the time of His Second Coming and of the end of the world, which He spoke of in His dissertations. Jesus gave His followers many signs that will precede His Second Coming at the end of the ages. The scriptures record these words: *"And there shall be signs in the sun, and in the moon."* [59]

Celestial Signs

Solar eclipses and total lunar eclipses [blood moons] in the last days give clues to the eminent spiritual events of the rapture and the return of Jesus. The prophet Joel prophesied that the sun will be turned dark and the moon will be blood-red at the time when the Lord comes.[60] John also prophesied that the sun will be darkened and the moon appears as blood at the time of the second coming of the Lord.

During His last week on earth, Jesus sat on Mount Olives surrounded by His disciples. He briefed them on the events preceding the last days of Gentile rule. He told them that there will be signs in the sun, the moon, and the stars, prior to the coming of the Son of Man. Regarding His return for His followers – the church, Jesus told them pointedly that immediately after the tribulation at that time, the sun will be darkened and the moon will not give her light. Here, Jesus revealed that He will appear in the skies at the time of a solar eclipse.

There were hundreds of blood moons and darkened sun since Daniel prophesied of the great tribulation in the last days. To date, none of those celestial signs related to the return of Jesus. How then can one identify the time of the end by the sign of a blood moon and a solar eclipse?

Three elements must come into play for a positive identification of the time of the end. These elements are the prophetic word, the fulfilling event, and the celestial sign. The celestial sign in close proximity to the event is a divine validation of the prophecy and its consummation. This pattern has been demonstrated in the re-birth of Israel as prophesied by Ezekiel. The time of the end will be identified in like manner.

Daniel prophesied that the last seven years will begin with the firm endorsement of an international treaty. This is the first element. Israel will not be a party to the negotiations, but they will be impacted by the outcome. Knowledge of the predicted treaty is the second element in solving the mystery. It is a huge challenge to identify that predicted treaty. The third element is the celestial sign at or close to the time of the signing of the treaty.

No one knows the day or the hour when Christ will return nor when the world will end. However, scriptures make it plain that God will do nothing without revealing His secret plans to His servants the prophets. Accordingly, God revealed a key component to the time of the end to the prophet Daniel. The events that will usher in the last years of Gentile Rule and the final punishment of the Jews were prophesied by Daniel twenty-five centuries ago. The prophecy declared that a prince shall make a firm agreement with many (nations) for a period of seven years.

Daniel gave clues regarding the mystery of the time of the end. He set the date of the signing of the treaty for the beginning of the seven years of the last days of the era. Without a doubt, the celestial signs referenced by Jesus will occur within those seven years.

False Prophets

The first sign Jesus told His followers to look for was the spiritual impersonators and spiritual deceivers. Many people will come using the name of Jesus and even claiming to be the Messiah. Those false messiahs will gain a following and lead many believers astray. This sign is already fulfilled. There are many false prophets and prosperity teachers today who attract large followers. They deceitfully use the name of Jesus and the word of God to fleece the flocks and amass extraordinary wealth to themselves.

There are many examples of those false teachers and prophets who deceived their followers and destroyed them. Foremost of those deceivers are Jim Jones, pastor of the Peoples Temple of California, America, and cult leader, David Koresh. Jones led hundreds of his faithful followers to Jonestown, Guyana, and built a religious colony in the jungle.

One fateful day after preaching, Reverend Jones gave his flock a deadly potion to drink and watched as they slumped to the ground and died. That massacre took place on November 18, 1978. Then there was David Koresh, self-proclaimed prophet, and leader of the Branch Davidian church in Waco, Texas. He and hundreds of his followers perished in an inferno in 1993 when their church buildings exploded.

Civil disturbances and wars.

Jesus predicted that there will be many wars and uprisings leading up to the time "There will be wars and rumors of wars"[61] Jesus warned. There have been more wars on earth over the past twenty years than at any other time in history. There have been major wars in Iraq, Afghanistan, wars in Syria, Yemen, Somalia; conflicts in Asia, Pakistan, India, and many wars in Africa. There were uprisings in many countries in the Arab world code-named Arab Spring. These conflicts prove that the sign of wars and rumors of wars has been fulfilled.

Famine

Jesus also predicted severe food shortages. He said that "There will be famines in various parts of the world".[62] The world's food supply is adversely affected by many factors. These include overpopulation requiring more food, wars, and the disaster caused by climate change. The earth gets warmer and climate pattern shifts cause millions of acres of fertile lands to become deserts. Less fertile lands result in lower production of food.

The State of food security in the world as reported by the world organization gives a shocking assessment of the hunger status of the world. The 2014 report states that eight hundred and five million people suffer from hunger. This translates to one out of every nine people in the world is affected by famine. This shocking state of the world's food supplies and widespread hunger is proof that the second coming of Jesus is near.

Earthquakes

Jesus predicted that there will be numerous earthquakes in various parts of the world at the time of the end. The fulfillment of the sign of many earthquakes is observed with clarity today. The United States Geological Survey National earthquake information center reported a mind-boggling number of over 230,000 earthquakes of magnitude 4.0–9.1 around the world between 2004 and March 2020. This puts the frequency of occurrence of magnitude 4.0 earthquakes at 30 a day. This number would be about fifty per day or higher if smaller tremors were included.

In the past ten years, there were more powerful earthquakes of magnitude 8.0 and above than there was in the last century. In recent years, earthquakes have caused a tremendous number of fatalities and billions of dollars of structural damages. The earthquake in the city of Bam, Iran, on December 26, 2003, killed 33,819 people. The tsunami which resulted from an earthquake near Indonesia, in the Indian Ocean on December 26, 2004, killed 227,898.

The earthquake in China in 2008 killed 87,587, and on January 12, 2010, a powerful earthquake left 320,627 dead in Haiti. A total of more than one million people has been killed by earthquakes since the beginning of the 21st century. The tremendous number of earthquakes and their intensity and frequency is an absolute proof of the fulfillment of the prophecy of Jesus.

Ungodliness

Many nations have rejected God. Recent research polls indicate about 31% of the world's population (2.235 billion) recognize Jehovah God and Jesus Christ, the Son of God. This group includes Christians and Jews.

The rest of the world (69%), which amounts to 5.175 billion people worship other gods. This group includes the major religions of Islam with the worship of Allah with no recognition of Jesus Christ as Lord and Savior. There are also the idol-worshippers (Hinduism, and Buddhism), and many smaller religions whose object of worship is animals, rivers, and the sun. There is also a great falling away from the Christian faith. Many professed Christians renounce their faith and re-enter the secular world of ungodliness.

Sexual misconduct

Ungodly people have become wicked on the earth; and it appears that the inclination and human thinking are continuously evil. Man has violated every law of God and scoffs at His revealed word. Modern man has rejected God's moral and spiritual standards. Thereby man has become an entity unto himself and creates his own laws based on what he deems to be right in his eyes.

Man has flagrantly violated God's holy law of marriage, which existed from the day that He created the first man and woman. God's law that marriage is between a man and a woman can never change. This law was affirmed by Jesus two thousand years ago. Jesus said, "That at the beginning the Creator made them male and female."[63] And for this reason, a man is united to his wife in marriage. Marriage was ordained by God at the beginning and is therefore a holy estate. The divine plan for the male and female in a union was to reproduce children. This procreation plan was designed to eventually produce the seed of the woman, who would crush the head of Satan.

Satan, the adversary, came up with a counter plan in an effort to hinder God's procreation plan, which leads to the birth of the Savior. Satan's plan was homosexuality, which guarantees infertility. Satan projected this so that the seed of the woman could not be produced and God's plan would be defeated. Homosexuality is an evil plan hatched by the Devil. Of a surety, homosexuality is an offense and a rebellion against God and His plan of procreation.

Therefore, the Lord condemns homosexuality, lesbianism, and all unnatural sexual misconducts. More so, the scriptures call out homosexuality as an abhorrent, detestable, and an abomination.[64] Consequently, any marriage apart from that which is based on the holy scriptures is ungodly and spiritually illegitimate, and is a transgression of the word of God.

Other Signs

Jesus gave many more signs of the end. He said that godly-believers will be hated by the ungodly people. They will be abused, persecuted, imprisoned and some will be killed for adhering to the gospel and faith in God. Lawlessness will abound in the nations, and iniquity will be multiplied, and people will become heartless, wicked, callous, and hateful. A good sign that the end is near is the outreach of the gospel to every nation. The scriptures declare that the message of salvation will be preached in every country as a testimony to the world before Christ returns.

Jesus gave all those signs, but with no indication of any specific date for the end. However, He gave the following clue which leads to a definitive timeline to the end. Jesus made a direct reference to Daniel's prophecy concerning the abomination of desolation or the desecration of the holy place, which undoubtedly is a reference to Temple Mount.

"So, when you see the appalling sacrilege spoken of by the prophet Daniel, standing in the Holy Place, [and] let the reader take notice and ponder and consider and heed [this]".[65] Clearly Jesus was not referencing the past abominable acts by the Antiochus Epiphanies who ruled Judah 175-164 BC. At that time, Antiochus committed the ultimate outrage of desecrating the Temple by erecting a statue of their Greek god, Zeus, and sacrificed a pig in the Temple.

Jesus was predicting an event far in the future which will give a point of reference for time of the end of the era; and the time of His second coming. That point of reference is the date of the signing of a future seven-year agreement between the prince, and many other nations.

Prophetically, we are in the last days. This is evidenced by the fact that many of the signs of the end that Jesus predicted are now fulfilled. At this point in history any treaty that satisfies Daniels requirements, could qualify as the end-time prophetic treaty: and the date of the signing of such treaty is the key to unlock the mysteries of the last days.

CHAPTER 12

PESTILENCE

Jesus declared that there will be pestilences in different places prior to His appearing. John, the revelator also prophesied that God would send pestilence as judgment upon the world in the last days. This was highlighted in the Seals and Trumpet judgments.

Over the past twenty years many deadly epidemics have infected millions all over the world. The yearly influenza kills thousands every year. Then new plagues suddenly appear at intervals of time.

The SARS and MEARS, and the H1N1 were deadly respiratory viruses of recent years; and the debilitating West Nile Virus and Dengue Fever infecting millions around the world. Then came the dangerous Ebola disease that struck multiple thousands with deadly vengeance.

A few months ago, in December, 2019, a brand-new respiratory infection appeared in China. The virus named coronavirus is highly transmissible, and deadly. The virus exploded into a global pandemic in a way that's unprecedented, says Dr. Anthony Fauci, America's top infectious disease expert.

At the present time, there is no vaccine, and no medication to control the spread of the virus. Subsequently, the coronavirus is the most frightening of all viruses over the past one hundred years. Everyone is at risk, warns Dr. Fauci.

The coronavirus disease named Covid-19 was first diagnosed in Wuhan, China, on December 8, 2019. The corona virus is a lethal pathogen which has infected every country on Earth. In the absence of a vaccine and an effective medication; Epidemiologists predicted that this virus is poised to ravage the nations. According to a recently published article: one Harvard scientist Marc Lipstich, predicted that covid-19 will likely infect 40-70% of the world's population, which is about 3 billion to five billion people.

Another biostatistician, Ira Longini, who advises the World Health Organization predicted that two thirds of the world's population may get covid-19. This percentage is calculated to be five billion people. Another public health scientist from Hong Kong, Prof. Gabriel Leung estimated that if the transmission rate of 2.5 additional people for each infected person is accurate, then 60-80% of the world's population could be infected. This results in 4.5-6 billion people infected.

The virus spreads rapidly over the world like an unchecked wildfire. The deadly pathogen, Covid-19 was declared a pandemic within 90 days of the first confirmed infection. During that time frame Covid-19 infected thousands of people in 160 countries. The world Health Organization and health departments across the world scrambled to deal with this deadly pestilence. People panicked in fear as the plague overwhelmed hospitals with the sick and dying victims.

This Covid-19 is a new disease which caught the world off guard. The virus is very virulent. Highly contagious and lethal. Once the virus enters the body it goes to the lungs. There it multiplies rapidly, and causes viral pneumonia. The lungs get filled with fluid which blocks oxygen from getting into the blood circulatory system. Consequently, the heart and other vital organs are starved of oxygen. The patient then becomes critically ill, and without appropriate medical intervention, death comes rapidly. Millions are infected, and hundreds of thousands have died within six months of the outbreak of the virus, and at this time, there seems to be no end in sight.

There are no medications, and no vaccines are presently available to fight this deadly pestilence. Health experts and scientists concluded that the only way to control the contagion is by mitigation. Their plan is to slow down the plague, and hope for a vaccine and medication to cure the disease. The plan calls for both government and citizen's participation. The government must do contact tracing, quarantine of suspected cases, widespread testing of the asymptomatic, isolation and hospitalization, and order a temporary lockdown of all non-essential businesses.

The government is also responsible to provide all the necessary personal protective equipment for hospitals and all agencies that work with covid-19 patients. All citizens were asked to practice social distancing, proper personal hygiene, frequent hand-washing, use facial covering, comply with stay at home order, and cover the mouth with the elbow when coughing and sneezing. Full participation by all parties is necessary for the plan to be effective.

The virus is no respecter of persons. Coronavirus is an equal opportunity pestilence. It attacks the very young and the very old, rich and poor alike, and it does not discriminate. It attacked world leaders, royalties, famous people and the average people with the same vengeance. Within four months of the first infection, over one million became infected in one hundred and sixty countries. Subsequently, over one hundred thousand died from the disease.

Coronavirus made a surprise attack upon a defenseless world and inflicted severe economic, and social damages. World leaders panicked. They were forced to lock down every country on Earth. The world's economies came to a screeching halt. Financial markets all over the world crashed, and caused trillions of dollars loss to investors.

Many countries closed their borders. Factories closed, all production lines come to a halt, and all nonessential businesses closed. Airplanes flew without passengers and public transportation ceased. Suddenly, millions of workers all over the world were furloughed as businesses shuttered their doors.

Many businesses went from boom to bust in a day. In short, the social and economic structures of the world suddenly collapsed, and plunged the world into chaos and uncertainty.

The world's economies were shattered. The nations of the world were defeated. Their powerful armies and navies were no match for the powerful impact of the lethal invisible covid-19 virus. There has never been a time when all the nations of the world were faced with such a dire crisis that caused all economies to simultaneously stop dead in their tracks.

This pandemic appears to be one which has markings of a supernatural intervention. It seems that a superior power flipped a switch, and instantly turned off the world's commerce, and sent governments into panic. It could well be that God, the Creator of the world, and of man, looked down from heaven, and was displeased with mankind.

The scriptures recorded that in times past, God sent pestilence upon people as punishment for awful transgressions. The Bible recorded that about 3,500 years ago, God sent plagues upon Egypt, which forced Pharaoh to release Israel from the bondage of the Egyptians. The Bible also recorded that God sent pestilence upon Israel, during the reign of King David, about 1000 BC. The plague was punishment for Israel because they committed a grievous sin against the Lord. "So, the Lord sent a pestilence upon Israel."[66] The plague was a deadly pathogen which killed 70,000 covenanted people in three days.[67]

The novel coronavirus pestilence of 2019-2020 could well be punishment for man's transgressions of the laws of God, and for the wickedness of mankind today.

Modern man has rejected God, and has rejected the commandments of God. Moreover, modern man has rejected the Holy Scriptures, rejected the fact that God created all things. Man has strayed far from God the Supreme Being. Modern man has ignored the divine purpose for which humanity was created.

God created man a little lower than the angels and set him as over-seer of the planet Earth.[68] The angels were ministering spirits, and man was created to worship God.

The scriptures reveal that man must "Fear God- know that He is, revere and worship Him- And keep His commandments; for this is the whole purpose of man."[69] Nonetheless, man has become an entity to himself. He flaunts the word of God, and overstepped the moral physical boundaries that the Creator has set for humanity.

Man rejects God's commands, and does what seems right in his own eyes. Man has violated all the moral laws of God. Now, man sets sight on violating the physical boundary law.

The Creator has given the Earth to man, but He reserved the heavens for Himself. Man's boundaries are the stratosphere surrounding the Earth. Beyond that point is the heavens. The Bible declares that, "The heavens are the Lord's heavens, but the Earth has he given to the children of men."[70] Yet, man sees the heavens as the last frontier.

On October 4, 1957, the Soviet Union violated God's law, and intruded into space. On that day, they successfully launched a satellite into space. The satellite named Sputnik was the first man-made object to enter space. The Soviets opened up a new frontier: and the world watched in awe as Sputnik orbited the Earth. Since that time there has been a mad rush by every advanced nation to explore the heavens.

Today, men and women live and work inside a space station. There are thousands of satellites whisking around in space even at this very moment. Man, now sets sight on a more ambitious plan to colonize planet Mars. All these acts are a clear violation of the word of God. Let the world know that God is alive. God is watching. God's word never changes. His word at the beginning of creation is the same today and forever.

The coronavirus pestilence could be a warning from God that man should change his ways. The nations should acknowledge the Creator. They should humble themselves and pray and turn from their wicked ways, and ask God to forgive their evil deeds, and heal their land. The word of the Lord as recorded in 2 Chronicles 17:14 are appropriate for this time and season. Like the great king Nebuchadnezzar, the nations must conclude that the Lord God is Sovereign, and rules from His Throne in Heaven: "And he does according to His will in the host of Heaven and among the inhabitants of the Earth; and none can stay His hand or say to Him, What are you doing?"[71]

The prophet Ezekiel wrote concerning the last days: "Thus says the Lord God: Behold I am against you, O Sidon, and I will show forth My glory and be glorified in the midst of you. And they shall know - understand – and realize that I am the Lord, when I execute judgments and punishments in her. For I will send pestilence in her."[72] This scripture rests squarely on the nations of the world today. The emergence of many deadly viral diseases over the past few years is proof that these are the last days as predicted by the Jewish prophets centuries ago.

CHAPTER 13

END IN SIGHT

The events leading up to the return of Christ are fast unfolding. Middle-East and world news indicated that the end is in sight. There has never been a time when there is so much evil and wickedness permeating throughout the nations.

Two thousand years ago, the Apostle Paul told the believers that they should not be disturbed or get anxious or excited about the signs of the time, or such gossip as to the time of the coming of the Lord. He then gave the church a pattern of events that will lead up to the time of the coming of Jesus.

The sequence of events leading up to the end are apostasy, extreme lawlessness, rebellion, revelation of the lawless man (Antichrist), and then the return of Christ. All the great nations today are impacted by lawlessness within their borders, and by terrorism.

The last days has been prophetically set, and as the time of the end approaches the Lord directs the minds of people to create events in order to fulfill His divine purpose, and accomplish His plans. God also opens the minds of His servants to understand the times and the seasons.

The scriptures reveals that the Lord decreed twenty-one acts of judgments upon the Earth to occur in the last days. These divinely purposed judgments code-named "Seals, Trumpets, and Vials" are spiritual symbols.

These judgments are vehicles which express the divine sentences manifested in the reality of the material world. They are prophetically fixed for the time of the end; and will take place over many years. Some of these judgments will precede the appearing of Jesus for the rapture of the church; while others will take place after the rapture, but before Jesus returns to Earth.

The judgments will be announced in the spiritual realm, but made manifest in the physical world. They will come in the form of natural disasters, unusual phenomena, wars, famines, and pestilences. These judgments will begin at the start of Daniel's 70th week, and continue through the great tribulation period. They will affect all people on Earth, and no one will escape the distress.

Seal Judgments

The plagues under the first seal will cause tremendous damage to the Earth's vegetation, water and atmosphere, and will affect every human being on the face of the Earth. The first seal was introduced as a symbolic white horse with a rider. The rider is a political and military leader. John describes him as an indiscriminate warrior who goes about capturing territories. The fulfillment of this seal is quite evident today as the world looks on as terrorist groups wage wars in Syria, Iraq, Yemen, Africa, and in Europe.

The second seal symbol presents a red horse and a rider who causes wars to break out because of his policies. This too appears to be in fulfillment as political instability consumes the Middle-East, and nations rise up against the terrorists.

The third seal was introduced as the black horse representing famine, while the fourth seal is introduced as a pale horse whose rider is death and destruction. Here, the prophet declares that the rider of the pale horse is a powerful potentate. He will declare war on his enemies. Eventually, many nations will be forced into battle. The prophecy states that a quarter of the Earth's population will be killed.

The fourth seal might well have been manifested in World War 2. The rider might well be Hitler, the powerful ruler of Germany. He started the war in which an estimated eighty million people died from the sword and from famine. The population of Europe and the Middle-East was regarded by the ancients as the Earth. The population of this region was estimated at four hundred million in 1939. Therefore, eighty million is within the bounds of a quarter of the population.

The fifth seal has a spiritual component, and begins immediately after the wars. Here, the prophet reveals the presence of multitude of souls in heaven, all dressed in white robes. These represent the spirits of righteous people who were killed during the time of the first four seals.

The sixth seal takes us back to Earth and reveals terrifying events. There will be a powerful earthquake, the sun will be darkened, and the moon will turn blood red. The lunar eclipse will be observed in the Middle-East, and shooting stars will fill the night skies.[73] The sixth seal has similarities with the seventh vial. They both display the wrath of God on evil men on Earth at the time of the end of the age.

Trumpet Judgments

The seventh seal will introduce the seven angels with the divine sentences of the trumpet judgments. The judgments of the seven trumpets will be even more damaging than the plagues of the seals.

The seal judgments, and the trumpet judgments will take place during the tribulation period; and seems to run in concurrence with the signs that were predicted by Jesus. These divine judgments against the Earth will cause severe distress, pain, suffering, death, and terror to the people on

Earth. These plagues will adversely affect climate, vegetation, water on land and the sea, and cause natural disasters of all kinds to ravish the Earth.

The Trumpet Judgments are divine sentences against wickedness on planet Earth. The first trumpet will deliver a storm of hail, and fire mingled with blood upon Earth. The severe heat wave caused by excessive powerful sun-flares coupled with global warming will cause a third of all the grass and trees on Earth to be burnt and destroyed.

The disastrous effect of the first trumpet judgment is evidenced by the adverse climate change that has a grip on the Earth today. Scientists reported that the Earth is getting warmer, the heat is melting glaciers, and the sea levels all over the world are rising. The weather pattern is greatly affected and large land masses are turning into deserts for lack of rain.

The effects of the second trumpet will be just as terrifying. A third of the sea will turn blood red, and a third of the sea creatures will perish, and a third of the ships on the seas will be destroyed. At the sound of the third trumpet, a star will fall from heaven upon the lakes and rivers, and a third of the lakes and a third of all freshwater on Earth will become poisoned. These are symbolic of things to come in the natural.

In the past few years, many rivers and lakes in different parts of the world mysteriously turned blood red over-night. There are reports that Rivers China, Russia, Africa, North America, and even Port Maria River in Jamaica suddenly turned red. The last large body of water to change color is the famous Lake Lonar in India. The 279-acre lake mysteriously turned red in one night in June 2020. This sudden change in color baffled scientists.

Apart from the mysterious changes in the waters, man is also creating havoc in Earth's water sources. The rapid growth of industries, and cities have caused many lakes, and rivers all over the world to be poisoned by industrial pollutants and sewage. This includes the largest bodies of fresh waters on Earth.

No water body is spared in man's quest of industrialization. The Great Lakes in North America are regarded as toxic soup, likewise Lake Victoria in Africa. Lake Karachay in Russia is a radioactive body. Likewise, many great rivers of the world are badly polluted.

The Mississippi River, Yellow River, King River in Australia, and the River of Johannesburg are just a few of the many that are so contaminated that anyone who drinks from them will fall ill, or die. The contamination of the world's fresh water proves that we are now under the third trumpet judgment. The fourth trumpet judgment will impact the sun, moon, and stars.

A third part of all the heavenly bodies will darken, and a third part of the day-time will darken. The fifth trumpet will deliver natural elements with terrifying effects. Dark smoke will be released into the atmosphere, and visibility will be so poor that the sun will not be seen. Then, suddenly, out of the darkness will come millions of demon-like locusts. They will swarm all over the Earth. This may be symbolic, but only time will tell.

The locusts will be very unusual; they will resemble horses dressed for battle, their heads will be covered with something that looks like golden crowns, their faces will have the appearance of people, they will have hair resembling that of a woman, and their teeth will look like that of a lion. Also, they will possess breast plates that look like they were made of iron, and they will have tails like scorpions with stings.

The locusts will be divinely forbidden to harm the grass or any herb or tree. Their assignments will be to attack people who do not have the mark of God on their foreheads. Their targets will be the ungodly and wicked people. They will not be permitted to kill anyone, but only to torment them with their venomous stings similar to that of a scorpion.

The duration of the fifth trumpet plague will be five months. The plague of the locusts will be so awful that people will cry out in agony under severe pain. Many will desire to die rather than bear the suffering, but death will elude them. The past year 2019 have seen locust swarms of biblical proportions. Millions of desert locusts destroyed millions of acres of food-crops in India and Africa, and farmers were helpless to stop the infestation, and crop destruction.

CHAPTER 14

RAPTURE OF THE REDEEMED

A few days before His crucifixion, Jesus made a solemn promise to His sorrowing disciples that He is going back to heaven. However, He will return and take them to heaven with Him. The early Christian believers also known as the church, were anxious for Jesus to return for them. The promised mass migration of believers to heaven is called the rapture of the church.

The first century believers were anxious for the return of Jesus. Many started speculating as to the time of Jesus' return for them. The Apostle Paul became aware of the speculations, and addressed the churches on the event of the return of Jesus. He wrote to church at Thessalonica and told them that the rapture will take place at the time of the first resurrection.

Christian believers today are just as anxious for the rapture as the early Christian. Today, there are diverse views among Christian denominations on the time of the rapture. Some pre-millennialism scholars teaches that the rapture will take place at any moment; and the prevailing view among many believers is that the rapture will take place before the tribulation.

A second belief among some Christian denominations is a "mid-tribulation rapture," and a third school of belief is that the rapture will take place at the end of the tribulation. Pre-millennialists have a choice of a pre-tribulation rapture, a mid-tribulation rapture, or a post-tribulation rapture.

These beliefs are at best pure speculations. Scriptures do not support the idea that Christ can return at any given moment. However, the Christian should live with the expectation that Christ will return for the church. With that in view, the believer should strive to live righteously at all times. He should display Christian character at all times. Not just a moral character, or legal correctness, but to manifest the fruit of the Spirit.

The fruit of the Spirit are the nine graces that sets the Christian apart from the secular person. These graces are the work of the presence of the Holy Spirit in the life of the believer. These characteristics are: love, joy, peace, patience (forbearance), kindness, goodness (benevolence), faithfulness; meekness (gentleness, humility), and self-control.[74]

The believer should live a life that is pleasing and acceptable to God, bearing in mind that at death his eternal destiny is sealed. Should he die before the rapture, his soul will be at rest until the day of the rapture.

The Bible does not explicitly relate the rapture of the church with the great tribulation. However, one could garner inferences to the relationship of the rapture to the tribulation. In chapter six of the book of Revelation, John described a terrible scene of wars, famine, pestilence, and death. This scene describes the atrocities and distress of the great tribulation.

Thereafter, the fifth Seal was opened. John saw many souls under the altar. Those were the souls of believers who were killed during the tribulation because of their testimony, and for the word of God. Those souls cried out to God to judge the people who persecuted and killed them.

Then each of them was given "long and flowing festive white robe, and told to rest, and wait patiently for a little while longer, until the number should be complete of their fellow servants, and their brethren who were to be killed as they themselves have been killed."[75]

The scripture indicates that Christian believers will go through the tribulation. This narrative therefore debunks the ideas of a pre-tribulation rapture.

God works by a divine plan and a given purpose. The time of Christ's appearing is only partially revealed in scriptures. The time of the rapture will therefore take place at a divinely appointed time. Jesus taught that He will come like a thief in the night. He will come suddenly without advance notice, and He will leave swiftly with the faithful believers.

No person on Earth knows when the rapture will take place or when Christ will actually return to Earth. However, the scripture partially reveals significant clues as to the season when Jesus will return for the church.

John relates that at the sound of the seventh trumpet, the twenty-four Elders that minister about the Throne of God, reveal that the Lord has taken His great power and begin to reign over the Earth. (Revelation 11:17) This was a point in time towards the end of the great tribulation. The scripture also reveals that "The time has come for the judging of the dead, and for rewarding your servants the prophets, and the saints and those who reverence your name."[76] This narrative reveals that the first resurrection and the rapture will take place close to, or at the end of the great tribulation.

In another scene, John describes a great multitude of people decked in long flowing white robes. They stood before the Throne and before the Lamb with palm branches in their hands. There were 144,000 Jews, and people from every race and creed in the great company in heaven. The angel then told John that "These people are they that came out of the great tribulation".[77]

This is a scriptural proof that the church will go through the great tribulation, and should put to rest the erroneous belief of a pre-tribulation rapture.

Jesus told His followers that His appearing for the rapture of the church will only take an instant of time. Jesus described the event saying; "as the lightning cometh out of the east, and shineth even unto the west; so, shall also the coming of the Son of man be".[78]

CHAPTER 15

VISION OF THE RAPTURE

In a night vision, the author got a glimpse of what the rapture might be like. He dreamt that a war was in progress and he was being chased by a number of enemy soldiers. He eluded them by climbing up the side of a mountain. I looked to the crown of the hill, and saw a fenced property.

I moved quickly towards a huge gate in the fence, and I observed that there were guards at the gate; I was scared. The enemy was chasing me. They were closing in fast on me, and now there were soldiers in front of me. I was trapped! However, I decided to take a chance with the guards. I went up to the gate of the camp, and beckoned for help; and the camp guards let him in.

There were many people taking refuge in the camp. Suddenly, a large crowd rushed into the courtyard, and they were all looking towards the sky. I also rushed out to see what was causing that great commotion. So, when I looked up into the distant eastern sky, I saw what looked like a small crimson cloud in the distance.

The cloud seemed to move very rapidly like a flash of lightning. It moved in the direction of the camp, grew greatly in size and blanketed the entire sky. Because of its immense size, it appears to stand still for a little while as it passes over the camp. All the people who were there looking up, raised their hands and calling on the name of Jesus.

Suddenly, a few of the people started floating upwards towards the cloud. I looked as many people lifted off like neon-filled balloons. As I pondered if I was going to be left behind, I suddenly found myself floating upwards. I was the last one to rise and it was a great feeling of euphoria as I joined the great company in the sky.

As the rapture proceeded many who were left behind on the ground started crying, and shouting, and pleading to Jesus to take them up. Their cries were not answered, and they watched as the faithful ones disappeared into the clouds, and it sped away at the speed of light.

CHAPTER 16

CONDITIONS FOR CHRIST'S APPEARING

Jesus will return for the church in the last days. That period begins with the fulfillment of Daniel's seventieth week prophecy. The first day of the signing of the covenant between the Prince and many nations marks the beginning of the last days. This prophecy was fulfilled un-noticed by the Christian world in the year 2015.

In 2015, the dominant nations signed a nuclear arms treaty with Iran. The date of the confirmation of the treaty is the key to unlock the mysteries of the last days. That date also marks the fulfillment of Daniel's "Seventieth Week" prophecy; and the beginning of the final years of Gentile world supremacy. Sadly, the religious world failed to recognize the fulfillment of the confirmed covenant treaty.

The second condition calls for the fulfillment of all the predictions of Jesus concerning the last days. Jesus predicted that there will be celestial signs in the form of eclipses at the time of His coming. Eclipses are a common phenomenon. There will be many eclipses over time. However, the eclipses which will be connected to His return are the eclipse of the sun and the total eclipse of the moon; which must be observed from Jerusalem.

Finally, these celestial signs must occur within thirteen years after the signing of Daniel's prophetic treaty. The thirteen years comprises Daniel's seven plus six years four months and twenty days added by the angel.[79] This added time will extend the tribulation period to thirteen years, four months, and twenty days.

The celestial signs that fall within the prophetically revealed thirteen-year period are most significant in determining the possible time of the rapture, and the return of Jesus. Five years has expired since the signing of the treaty on July 14, 2015.

There may be eight years remaining until the end of the tribulation period. NASA predicted that there will be two partial lunar eclipses, one penumbra, and one total lunar eclipse [blood moons], and also two partial solar eclipses observable from Jerusalem, between July 2020 and July 2028. These celestial events cover the last eight years of the tribulation.

The eclipses will occur as follows: May 16, 2022 (partial lunar), May 5, 2023 (penumbra), September 18, 2024 (partial lunar), September 7, 2025 (total lunar), October 25, 2022, (partial solar), and August 2, 2027 (partial solar). [Credit: Fred Espenak, NASA].

These eclipses appear to satisfy Jesus 'celestial signs criteria for His return'. First, they will be observed from Jerusalem, at the place where Jesus was standing on Mount Olives. Secondly, they will occur in the prophetic last days-dating from July 14, 2015. Without a doubt, those future celestial events observable from Jerusalem are the key celestial signs referenced by Jesus during the discourse with His disciples on Mount Olives; and they will be manifest during thirteen years dating from 2015.

The Rapture is at Hand. Today, April 17, 2020, I dreamt that I was driving on a highway when a young man in a white sedan in the left land came alongside my car. Both cars came to a stop in the middle of the highway.

The young man called out my name, and handed me a neatly written note. The message reads, "JESUS IS COMING."

The Bible declares that the rapture is sure. This truth is undergirded by the word of the Lord. A few days before He was crucified, Jesus told His disciples that He is going away to prepare a place for them, and solemnly promised that He will return, and take them to heaven.[80] The scriptures gave a clear indication that the great and spectacular event will take place during the great tribulation. The glorious event will likely take place towards the latter end of the great tribulation. At that time, the nations in the Middle-East will be engaged in a brutal war.

CHAPTER 17

CAUGHT UP

At the time of the rapture, Jesus Christ will appear in the sky. He will be accompanied by a company of angels. Paul taught that the Lord will then send His angels with a great sound of a trumpet to gather His chosen ones – the Church, from the four corners of the Earth.[81]

The first angel will blow the resurrection trumpet, and summon all the saints who sleep in the graves. The Earth will tremble and shake, and graves will open, and the souls of the righteous dead will come forth. The souls will possess glorified supernatural bodies dressed in long white robes.

The seas will give up their dead, and those who are cremated will all appear in their new supernatural bodies. Resurrected saints will appear everywhere clothed in long flowing white robes. They will be seen coming out of homes and buildings, and walking through walls like walking through doors. They will be seen in the parks, on the streets, and everywhere.

The trumpet of God shall sound a second time. The time the living and faithful Christian believers who survive the ordeal of the great tribulation will be changed in an instant, from mortality to immortality. Like the resurrected saints, they will be given glorified supernatural bodies clothed in flowing white robes. Then in a flash, the resurrected saints and the living saints will rise from the ground, and take off like a rocket to meet the Lord in the air, who will take them to heaven.

The apostle Paul wrote concerning the rapture of the church: *"For this we say unto you by the word of the Lord, that we which are alive and remain (faithful) unto (until) the coming of the Lord shall not prevent them which are asleep. For the Lord Himself shall descend from heaven with a shout, with the voice of the archangel, and with the trump of God: and the dead in Christ shall rise first: Then we which are alive and remain (faithful) shall be caught up together with them in the clouds, to meet the Lord in the air: and so shall we ever be with the Lord."* [82]

Giving specific dates for the rapture is mere speculations. However, the scriptures reveal a possible period in which the Lord could return for the church. Yet, no one knows or will be able to correctly guess the time of the rapture.

Jesus said that He will come like a thief in the night, and at a time when no one expects. We are in the last days, and these are the predicted days for His appearing. Therefore, be like the wise virgins, and be spiritually ready at all times, to be caught up in the clouds to meet the Lord in the air.

The Last Days

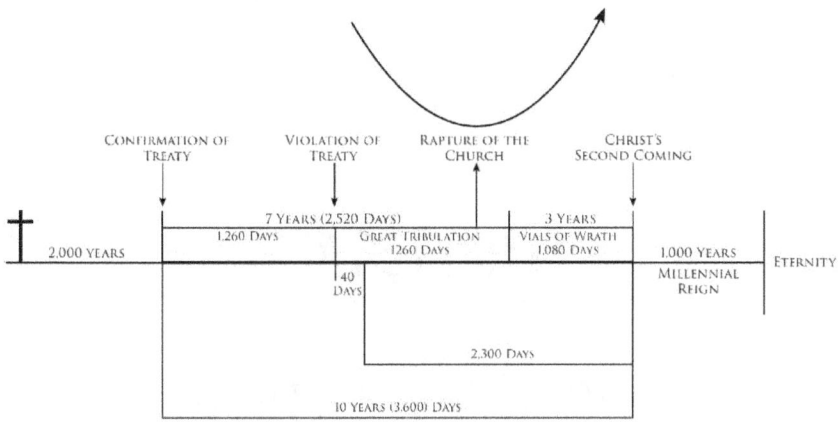

Diagram - Not to Scale

CHAPTER 18

MIDDLE-EAST CONFLICT

The sixth trumpet in John's vision of the last days, signals a call to battle. This indicates that a major world conflict is divinely decreed. The world is presently in disarray, and in total chaos. A global pandemic is sweeping throughout every nation of the Earth. As a result, many national economies have collapsed as a consequence of forced lock-down. Yet, many others are tethering on the brink of collapse.

A collapse of the world's social system is possible with dire consequences. People everywhere are very restive. Millions of people are taking to the streets and demanding change in social justice. There are protests and demonstrations against authorities in many countries.

The nations are on an edge. A global war seems inevitable. The scriptures reveal that the date and hour of the start of a major war is divinely appointed. John wrote that after the sounding of the sixth trumpet, a solitary voice commanded the angel to set loose the four death angels. Those angels were waiting by the Euphrates River for the date and time, to execute their order by striking the nations with war. Here is a clear indication that the next world conflict will begin in the Middle-East.

The next world conflict will be World War-3. From all indications, and according to John's vision, the Middle-East will host the first battle. The political conditions in the Middle-East is very unpredictable. There are wars to the north of Israel, and also in the eastern Levant. Meanwhile, there is the constant bickering of the Palestinians.

The Israeli/Palestinian peace negotiations is at a stalemate. The United States proposed a peace plan which was rejected by the Palestinians. The proposal as called for creating an eastern border for Israel whereby parts of the West-Bank territories will be annexed to Israel.

Israel will go boldly and unilaterally implement that peace plan. They will annex the West Bank as proposed. This unilateral Israeli action could take place in 2020, and this will cause consternation by the Palestinians. They will be furious, and would call for actions against Israel. The Muslim nations will rally to the cause of the Palestinians. Likewise, many nations that hate Israel will support the Palestinians cause.

Ezekiel prophesied that in the last days many nations in the Middle-East will join forces with a powerful northern nation. The ruler of Magog (Russia) will join forces with Gomer (Turkey), Persia (Iran), Libya, and Ethiopia.[83]

For the first time in history, the Russian armies have taken positions in the Middle-East at the invitation of Syria. Their reported objective is to support the Syrian Regime against insurgents. Notwithstanding, Russia has used this as a pretext to build a strong military presence in the Middle-East. They brought in warships, fighter jets, tanks, and every type of modern weapons into the region.

Presently, Russia has a huge naval base in Syria. They also have several military airfields in various parts of Syria. There are also thousands of Russian troops in bases in Syria. Some are at the doorsteps of Israel, which is only a few miles from their northern border.

The presence of Russian military assets and thousands of troops scattered across Syria poses a threat to the region. Presently, the Israelis are fighting a proxy war against Iran. They are flying sorties against Iranian positions in Syria. There is much risk in those operations, as Israel may mistakenly attack Russian camps and cause much casualties. But on the contrary, this will cause the Russians to retaliate, and declare war on Israel.

The main objective of the Russians will be to overpower the Jewish nation, and eliminate them. With Israel out of the way, the Russians will have complete control of the Middle-East region with its vast oil reserves.

The Muslim nations will cease the opportunity to ally with Russia in a war against Israel, and this will be their golden opportunity to destroy the Jews. Their dream is to capture the land of Israel, and establish a Muslim nation that will finally come to pass. Their great plan of Muslim dominance of the entire Middle-East will be accomplished with the demise of Israel. With Israel vanquished, the Muslims will have total control of the vast stretch of lands from the Indian Ocean to the Atlantic Ocean. Consequently, the entire Middle-East, and North Africa with a land mass greater than the continent of Europe will be controlled by Muslim nations.

CHAPTER 19

INVASION OF ISRAEL

Scriptures reveal that in the last days, the Lord will gather the nations to declare war on Israel.[84] Twenty-six hundred years ago, the prophet Ezekiel prophesied that in the last days of present-day Russia, many Muslim nations will invade the land of Israel. Signs of the times indicates that these are the last days of the present era (Common Era).

Given the tenuous political situation in the region, a war against Israel could break out within months, thereby fulfilling Ezekiel's prophecy. Currently, Russian troops are already at the door-step of Israel. They are positioned in Syria; observe that southern Syria borders Israel.

There are thousands of Russian troops presently in Syria. The Russians have several military airbases and outposts in easy striking distance of Israel. They also have the largest naval base in Syria, on the Mediterranean Sea, positioned at less than two hundred miles from Israeli shores.

The prophet predicted that present day Turkey, Iran, Libya, and Ethiopia will join forces with Russia and invade Israel. The combined armies assembling to fight against Israel will comprise of elite units from other

Muslim nation as well as their proxy forces, and the Palestinians forces will also rise up against Israel.

The Russian led armies will attack from land, sea, and air. The invaders will come from the north, east, West, and south. Moreover, the Palestinians will attack from the West Bank.

The prophet also predicted that the invaders will come like a storm, and cover the land like a cloud. Israel will face perilous times; they will be overwhelmed, and overpowered. The survival of the Jewish nation will be in the balance. Defeat will mean the end of the nation. Therefore, they have no option but to fight to the death.

However, Israel will not be alone. Any invasion of Israel will be the flashpoint for a major Middle-East war. Attack on Israel, by the Russian led coalition forces will trigger World War-3.

The United States and her allies will respond with force in defense of Israel. The war will eventually take on a global nature. Within a few months, all the nation on Earth will be engaged in a global war- World War-3.

CHAPTER 20

BATTLE FOR JERUSALEM

Scriptures has revealed that the Lord will gather the nations to fight against Israel.[85] This will be the second battle against Israel in World War 3.

The purpose of this divinely decreed conflict was twofold. Firstly, it will fulfill Jeremiah's prophecy of "Jacob's Troubles." The war will also serve as a form of punishment to the Jews for their transgressions and atrocities while they were under the influence of the Antichrist. Secondly, the war will give legitimacy for destroying the heathen nations that seek to destroy Israel.

Meanwhile, the global war continues. Those nations that has developed massive hatred for Israel will be furious because the Jews defy the United Nations, and annexed the West Bank, and build their temple on Temple Mount. Those nations will gather to fight against Israel.

The mighty coalition armies will gather at a staging ground in the plains of Megiddo, Israel. The coalition forces will number in the millions. They will be so numerous that the scriptures predicted that they will charge upon the mountains of Israel as a storm, and cover the land like a cloud. The prophet Joel described the invading armies as hostile and mighty, the like of which has never been before, nor ever will be in the future.[86]

The battles will rage with fury on the mountains of Israel. The invading armies will prevail. They will over-run villages and towns, and capture and destroy many cities as they march towards Jerusalem. The Israelis forces will fight valiantly, but will be no match to the powerful, and numerous invading armies. They will be forced to retreat to Jerusalem. The enemy will surround the city and besiege it for many days.

Daniel prophesied that the time of the invasion of Israel in the last days will be "a time of trouble, (distress) such as never was since there was a nation even to that same time."[87]

Jeremiah prophesied that this will be the time of "Jacob's Troubles."[88] These will be the days of panic, trembling, terror, and no peace. The prophet Zechariah prophesied about the plight of the Jews. He wrote that the people of Jerusalem will be subjected to horrendous conditions during that war. They will be persecuted, oppressed, afflicted, and distressed. Jesus referred to this time of distress as the time of the great tribulation.[89]

Jesus warned that that period will be the time of great tribulation, and those will be days of great affliction, distress, and depression; such as never occurred since the world was created and never will be again.[90]

Zechariah prophesied that the enemy will capture Jerusalem with overwhelming force. The invading soldiers will plunder the houses. They will terrorize the people and rape the women. The Jewish nation will face their worst fears - a devastating defeat, and possible extinction.

The invading armies will inflict heavy casualties on Israel. They will kill two thirds of the Israeli population in their rampage throughout the country, according to scriptures.[91] The casualties could reach 6,000,000 dead. Also, half of the residents of Jerusalem will be taken into captivity. Moreover, the invaders will take control of Jerusalem.[92]

CHAPTER 21

ANTICHRIST COMES TO JERUSALEM

While the horrors of World War-3 are in progress, the Great Leader, referenced in scriptures as the Little Horn, and the Beast, and in religious circles as the Antichrist, will enter Jerusalem

The Antichrist will enter Jerusalem as the conquering general. The leaders of Jerusalem and great men will respect him, but many great men and some priests, and rabbis will show apprehension. They will distrust the Antichrist, and protest his presence in Jerusalem. The Antichrist will not tolerate anyone who opposes him, as all dissenters will pay a heavy price. The Antichrist will persecute them and put them in prison to silence them.

The Antichrist will make great speeches and gloat with pride, and will magnify himself above all men, and even declare that he is as great as Messiah. He will pervert and seduce the people with flatteries. Furthermore, he will profane the holy sanctuary, and will abolish the daily sacrifice, and demand that the people pay him homage.

The Antichrist will commission a statue of himself to be erected, which is totally against the Jewish religion. Consequently, the people will willingly fall into idolatry. Because of the ungodliness and rebellion of the people, God will give both the people and the sanctuary over to the Antichrist, to be trampled underfoot.[93] As a result, righteousness and truth will be cast down to the ground.

This period of irreligiousness and wickedness was described by Daniel, and will begin when the Antichrist profane the holy sanctuary.[94] The angel told Daniel that the desolation, anguish, atrocity, and abomination will begin at that point, and continue for two thousand and three hundred days. However, the daily sacrifice will resume after one thousand two hundred and ninety days.[95]

Two important visitors will also enter Jerusalem at about the time when the Antichrist made his entry. They are God's two witnesses to truth, and righteousness. Those two evangelists will be dressed in strange garments

Those two evangelists were divinely assigned to Israel for a period of forty-two months; during the time of desolation, and atrocity under the Antichrist. Their major mission will be to turn the hearts of the Jews to God, before the return of Jesus Christ the Messiah.[96]

The destruction of the Jewish nation by the gentile armies did not surprise the Lord. He knows the end of all things from the beginning. This war and the outcome were prophesied about twenty-six hundred years earlier by Ezekiel, Daniel, and other prophets. Jesus also confirmed the plight of the Jews when he warned about the great tribulation.

The Lord permitted the punishment of the Jews because of their unbelief, and rejection of the Covenant. The scriptures made it plain that the Lord permitted and allowed the misfortune of Israel in the last days. Zechariah wrote, "For I will gather all nations against Jerusalem to battle; and the city shall be taken, and the houses rifled, and the women ravished; and half of the city shall go forth into captivity, and the residue of the people shall not be cut off from the city."[97]

Let it be clear, the Lord did not abandon his people Israel. On the contrary, Israel abandoned their God in the last days. The judgment against Israel was to bring them to the place of repentance. The scriptures state that the Lord will put the surviving third part of the Jews through the fire, in order to refine, and to purify them, and to prepare their hearts to receive Messiah.

Defeated and dejected, they became helpless, and in a hopeless place. The remnant of Israel faced utter destruction. Military power failed. Their allies did not come to their aid. The Lord is their only hope for national survival. A broken and contrite nation will humble themselves and pray. Destitute, broken, and in their distress, they will call on the name of the Lord.

The remnants of the Jews will go through the proverbial fire. Their faith in God will be tried. They will have no one to turn to in their time of great trouble. Terrified and distressed, they will remember their God. They will repent of their transgressions, and in supplication and prayer, they will cry out to the Lord for help.

The Lord will hear their cry and answer them. He will acknowledge them, and show mercy and grace. He will say, "It is my people: and they shall say, The Lord is our God."[98] The scriptures revealed that the Lord will be furious against the invading nations.[99] The Lord will intervene in the affairs of man. He will use his mighty power to defend His people, Israel.

CHAPTER 22

WORLD WAR-3 UNRELENTING

The sixth trumpet judgment will continue in its manifestation as World War-3. The war will be unrelenting throughout the world, even after the battle of Jerusalem.

Nations will be fighting for their survival. They will defend themselves with every weapon at their disposal. They will deploy weapons of mass destruction of every kind. Nations will use chemical weapons, biological weapons, and even display nuclear weapons.

The scriptures state that the weapons will be nothing like what existed at that time. The prophet predicts that the weapons of the last days will shoot smoke, brimstone, and fire. This is a good description of the explosive effects of modern weapons. Bombs, rockets, and shells all give off fire and smoke. Undoubtedly, weapons of mass destruction will be deployed. Chemical weapons, and nuclear arms will come into play. Consequently, many cities will be completely ruined.

Biological and nuclear weapons will be deployed by some nations. This will trigger uncontrollable global pandemics. Communicable diseases will break out all over the world with no vaccines or medications to contain them. Modern weapons of rockets, missiles, tanks, war planes, and advanced guns will cause catastrophic damages world-wide. All three plagues – wars, famine, and pandemics – will be happening at the same time.

The great tribulation, and the global wars will take a gut-wrenching toll on humanity. There will be severe food shortages, and famine will rage across the world as a consequence of a vicious, and prolonged world war.

As a result, the social and economic conditions on Earth will be unbearable. Millions on every continent will live in fear and dread. Sufferings and death will be everywhere. John, the revelator wrote that a third of the world's population will perish as a consequence of the plagues. Given the current world population, the death toll could number more than two billion people.

The destruction of cities, the famine, the pandemics, the carnage, and barbarism of nation against nation, and man against man will be too much to bear. Man will reach the point of despair. A point where he will have lost all sense of reasoning. Man will reach a point of desperation, hopelessness, and gloom.

There will be no clear winner of the war. All nations will be destroyed, and all will be losers. At that point, evil thoughts will enter the minds of the commanders of the armies. They will plan to recklessly use all their nuclear weapons, and biological weapons of mass destruction on their enemies. Without a doubt, such callous acts could cause a nuclear winter that will destroy all living things.

The Lord knows the mind of man, and He will draw the line. He will take action to prevent man from destroying his creation. He will end the war and the great tribulation.

Jesus told His disciples that conditions on Earth at the time of the end will be so calamitous that God will cut the tribulation short so as to save humanity from total destruction.[100]

CHAPTER 23

ANGELIC PRONOUNCEMENTS

The Lord will not be oblivious to the devastation on Earth. The great tribulation is no surprise to God, neither is the catastrophic war. The scriptures revealed that everything that will occur on Earth in the last days was decreed, and affirmed by the prophets.

God is omniscient, and therefore knows all things that happened in the past, in the present, and all things that will happen in the future. The scriptures declare that God knows the end from the beginning, and all things are done according to His will and purpose.

Seventh Trumpet

In the last days, while the plague of war is wreaking havoc upon the Earth, and while the nations celebrate their great victory over Israel in the battle of Jerusalem; John the revelator directs us to a scene in heaven. There, John gives us a glimpse of the spiritual machinations at the time of the end.

John recalled that a mighty angel came forward and blew the seventh trumpet, and made three great pronouncements. He revealed to John that the first resurrection will take place during the days of the sounding of the seventh trumpet. The angel said that the righteous will be judged, and rewards will be given to the servants of God and to the saints.[101]

Secondly, the time will come when the Lord will destroy the people that destroyed the Earth.

Thirdly, at the sounding of the trumpet, the heavenly hosts declare that God now takes authority over the nations on Earth. John wrote that great voices in heaven declares that, "The kingdoms of this world are become the kingdoms of our Lord, and his Christ; and he shall reign for ever and ever."[102]

God is the creator and ruler of the universe. However, in the beginning, God created Adam and gave him dominion over the Earth. God then assigned him the responsibility to protect and maintain the Earth.[103]

Many centuries later, God affirmed man's dominion over the Earth. After the great floods in the days of Noah, God instituted human government, and empowered man to rule on His behalf over man in an organized society. The highest authority given to man entails capital punishment, after due course under law.[104]

Over time, the power to rule over the nations was passed exclusively into the hands of the gentile race. Nonetheless, the entire Adam's race failed miserably in their divine assignment. Throughout the ages, man sought to rule for himself and not for God. The result was chaos and destruction.

At this time, the Lord will withdraw the dominion and authority from man. The times of the Gentiles will then come to an end, and world domination by super powers will finally cease.[105]

CHAPTER 24

INVESTITURE OF THE KING

Heaven now prepares Christ to return to Earth, and strip man of authority and dominion over planet Earth, and rule as king. However, Christ must first have a nation. Secondly, He must be invested as king in a manner according to earthly tradition.

Two thousand years ago, Christ came to Earth as the son of David, and heir to the throne of Israel. He was declared king by the Roman governor, but was rejected by the Jews. Nevertheless, He was crowned with thorns, and mocked, and derided by the heathens.

He was crucified, died, buried and was resurrected, and returned to heaven. Israel is His earthly country according to the scriptures. He will be coming back to Israel to rule from Jerusalem after His investiture.

A ceremonial event will begin in heaven following the first sounding of the seventh trumpet. That event is the divine investiture of Christ. The dictionary defines investiture as a ceremony in which honors or rank is formally conferred on a person.

The person already had the prescriptive rights to the position. Therefore, the ceremony is merely an act of formally investing the person with the honors. A prime example is the succession to the throne in a monarchy.

In our time, Queen Elizabeth 11 ascended the throne, and began her rule on February 6, 1962 but was not formally enthroned until June 2, 1953.

In like manner, Christ is ruler of the heavens and the Earth. He rules from heaven, but will be coming into the material world to rule as King of the Jews, and king over the nations of the world.

A heavenly ceremony will therefore take place in which Jesus Christ is formally invested as King, and ruler of the kingdoms of the Earth. John wrote that the seventh angel who stood before God came forth with his trumpet. He raised the trumpet to his lips and blew.

Immediately after the sounding of the trumpet there were loud voices in heaven saying, *"the kingdoms of this world are become the kingdoms of our Lord and His Christ; and He shall reign forever."*[106]

Then the twenty-four elders [angels] that sit before God fell prostrate before Him and worshipped. They declared that the Lord God Omnipotent has now taken His great power and begun to reign over the Earth.

Daniel prophesied that power and authority and glory will be given to the Son of Man [Christ], and that all people, and nations, and languages shall serve Him. Moreover, His dominion, power, and authority will not be temporary like that of the Gentiles, but His kingdom shall endure forever.

At the time of sounding of the seventh trumpet, and the moment of the investiture, Christ becomes king of Israel. At that moment, He takes full power and authority over the nation, and begin His reign from heaven

CHAPTER 25

BATTLE OF ARMAGEDDON

The first act of Christ the King will be to engage the nations in battle. The Lord will summon the nations to gather at Armageddon. This place is a hill rising from the plains of Megiddo in northern Israel.

World War-3 will still be in progress as the troops march to Armageddon. A massive army will gather at Armageddon. That army will represent fighting units from many nations. Battle lines will be drawn. The battle will be between Christ the Lord, and the nations that come against Israel. The battle will take place after the fall of Jerusalem.

At Armageddon, God will aim to destroy the nations that come against Israel.[107] He will display His indignation and fury against the nations for destroying the Earth, and for their maltreatment of His people, Israel. Furthermore, God will take retribution against the nations for scattering the Jews among the heathens, and for depriving Israel of their divine rightful inheritance.

Today, the land of Israel is divided, and the city of Jerusalem parted among many Gentile nations. Consequently, the Lord takes vengeance against the nations for dividing up His land - Israel.[108] Finally, the battle is the way in which God will choose to cut short the great tribulation, and end the distress and oppression of the masses.

The battle of Armageddon will be the greatest battle of all times. There was no battle like that since Adam, and there will be no more like it after. This will be the final battle of the ages (Common Era).

On one side will be the nations of the world that hate the Jews. Their armies will be powerful, and number in the millions. Their commander in chief will be the Antichrist. This mighty world army represents malevolence, pride, and ungodliness. On the other side will be Christ the King, the commander of the heavenly forces.

The contest begins when the seventh angel with the seventh vial with the last judgment, raises the vial, and pours out the contents in the air. Immediately, thereafter, a mighty voice resounded out of the sanctuary from the throne of God saying, "It is Done!"[109] The judgments are pronounced.

The contents of the seventh vial are immediately manifested on Earth with catastrophic effects. There were blinding flashes of lightning, and loud rumblings, and peals of thunder, and a tremendously powerful earthquake struck the Earth.

No earthquake of such magnitude has ever occurred on Earth since man was created. The earthquake was so powerful and far-reaching that the whole planet rumbled, and tremored. Apparently, many of Earth's tectonic plates suddenly shifted simultaneously, releasing massive amounts of energy with catastrophic results.

The scriptures recorded that the great city (Babylon-New York City) was broken in three parts, and many cities of the nations collapsed. Many mountains were moved by the powerful seismic waves. Some mountains were dislodged from their foundations, and broken down, creating new valleys, hills and plains.

The scriptures gave an example of one such places of occurrence. The Mount of Olives shall split open from east to west. Half of the mountain shall move northwards, and half move southwards. Consequently, new lands and a great valley will be formed, stretching from the Jordan River to the Mediterranean Sea.[110]

The scriptures further revealed that the earthquake will demolish the mountains surrounding Jerusalem. The mountain range running from Geba (Geva Binyamin), six miles north of Jerusalem, to Rimmon, about thirty-five miles to the south, which is part of the West Bank, will crumble, and fall. This land mass is occupied by Palestinian Arabs. Consequently, all the mountain lands occupied by Palestinians from Geba (Geva Binyamin) to the south of Israel will be turned into a large plain.

The mountains will crumble and fall, but the foundation of Jerusalem will not be moved. The city will remain firm in its place, unaffected by the earthquake, and will appear lifted up above the newly created plains.

Jerusalem will then be positioned on a high elevated peak, towering over the northern portion of the plains. Two rivers of living (moving) waters will flow from Jerusalem. One will flow west to the Mediterranean Sea, and the other will flow to the Dead Sea.[111]

The great earthquake will change landscapes, and reposition many river courses and lakes around the world. Many Islands disappear as a consequence of enormous tsunamis. The earthquake will effectively restructure the surface of planet Earth.[112]

The earthquake was only the first phase of the divine attack against the enemies of Israel. The shaking of the planet represents the ground attack. Next comes the attack from above. The scriptures revealed that numerous stones (meteorites) weighing between fifty and one hundred pounds will strike the earth with deadly force. These fiery missiles will destroy everything in their path. They will destroy buildings, ships, planes, tanks, all military equipment of the nations that fought against Israel.

The armies of the nations that gathered at Armageddon will be devastated. The great military leaders, kings, and people will cry in fear, and take refuge in caves, and hide behind rocks. The ungodly nations, and all those professed believers who missed the rapture, and left behind shall shake and tremble, and cry out in fear: because the indignation and the wrath of God is poured out upon them.

The Lord will defeat the nations in the battle of Armageddon, and subdue them, and utterly destroy their power. Thereby, Christ the King will put an end to the times of the Gentiles. The Lord will end the great tribulation, and close the Common Era by His great victory at Armageddon.

All the great nations will be ravaged, and weakened by the wars, famines and pandemics of the tribulation judgments. The political, economic, and military powers of the great nations will be broken. Humanity will become helpless, and societies will rapidly deteriorate at the failure of mankind. A broken and distressed people that survives the great tribulation will remember the Creator, and hope for, and gladly welcome a new world order.

CHAPTER 26

COMING AGAIN.

Jesus Christ will return to Earth at the end of the ages (Common Era). This fact is well recorded in the scriptures. Jesus spoke of His return with power and great glory.[113]

Angels testified, and affirmed that Jesus is coming again. Their testimony was made on the day Jesus went back to heaven; two thousand two thousand years ago.[114] Then, there is the testimony of the apostle John. He declared, "Behold He cometh with the clouds: and every eye shall see Him."[115]

The coming back to Earth of Jesus Christ is a universal belief among Christians throughout the ages. However, the time of His return is not revealed in scriptures. Jesus told His followers that no one knows the day nor the hour when the Son of Man will return to Earth. Nevertheless, the prophets predicted that the Lord will return at the end of the ages.

The term "end of ages" is synonymous with the term "the last days." The last days is defined as a divinely appointed period, beginning at the date of the signing of the covenant of Daniel's Seventieth Week prophecy. The date of the signing of that treaty is the key to unlock the mysteries of the last days. That date also marks the beginning of the final years of Gentile world supremacy.

The Iran nuclear deal treaty with the nations perfectly fits the criteria of Daniel's predicted covenant. That treaty was signed on July 14th, 2015. This is undoubtedly the reference date for the beginning of the end. The suggested time until the end is calculated by adding the angel's 2,300 days to Daniel's seven years (2,520 days).[116]

Christ's return will be in two stages. The first stage will be devoted to the church. Christ will appear in the sky like a flash of lightning from east to west. As He moves through the skies, the true believers in the church will be caught up to meet Him in the air. This event is called the rapture of the church. This will fulfill the promise to His followers two thousand years ago; that He will come and take them to heaven.

The second stage of Christ's return will be devoted exclusively to the people of Israel. Christ will return to Earth in accordance with the scriptures. At that time, He will fulfill God's promise to David. That divine promise was to establish David's house, and his kingdom forever.

Signs for the Second Advent

Jesus gave His followers specific signs that will occur at the time of His return. He also told His followers that He will come again immediately after the great tribulation. However, He revealed that the great tribulation will be cut short, but did not say by how much time. This makes it very difficult for anyone to know the time of His coming.

Jesus predicted that there will be a solar eclipse at the time of His return. He said that the Sun shall be darkened, and the Moon shall not give her light.[117]

The prophet Joel also prophesied concerning the Second Coming of Jesus. According to his prophecy, there will be an eclipse of the sun prior to the return of the Lord to Jerusalem. Joel wrote that, "The Sun shall be turned into darkness, and the Moon into blood, before the great and terrible day of the Lord."[118]

John, the revelator also described the event of a solar eclipse in the last days prior to the return of the Lord.[119]

The eclipse events give a good indication of the time of the Second Coming. Eclipses are not unusual celestial events. They occur quite frequently, and are observed at various times all over the world. These prophetic eclipses are similar in nature, but their occurrence is predetermined for a specific time and placement.

The predicted eclipses will occur within the time period of the last days. Specifically, they will occur before the end of the great tribulation, and will be observable from Jerusalem.

Jesus declared that He will return to Jerusalem immediately after the tribulation at the end of the age – the Common Era.[120] The Lord knows the future, and determines the times and the seasons. The time of His coming is hidden from the minds of men. He said that no one would know the day nor the hour when He will appear in the sky for the church, or the time of His coming back to Earth.

There are two main criteria for the consummation of Jesus predicted signs. First, the signs must be observed from Jerusalem. Note that all these selected celestial signs can be viewed from where Jesus was standing on Mount Olives.

Secondly, they must occur in the prophetic last days. The last days began at the signing of the Iran deal in 2015, and presumably will end in 2028. Without a doubt, those future celestial events observable from Jerusalem are the key celestial signs referenced by Jesus during the discourse with His disciples on Mount Olives. These signs will be made manifest during the thirteen-year period, dating from July 14, 2015.

Many years has expired since the signing of the treaty on July 14, 2015. Accordingly, there are only a few years remaining until the end of the full tribulation period, which is calculated to last 13 years.

NASA predicted that there will be two partial solar eclipses observable from Jerusalem, between July 2020 and July 2028. These celestial events will occur within the last eight years of the tribulation period. The eclipses will occur as follows: October 25, 2022, (partial solar), and August 2, 2027 (partial solar).[121]

The blood moons referenced by Joel and John will occur in September, 2025, and December, 2028. From all indications, those four predicted solar and lunar events are the only eclipses that will fall within the prophetically revealed thirteen-year period of the last days. However, the eclipse on August 2, 2027 perfectly fits the Bible criteria revealed by Jesus for the Second Coming.

The celestial clues that Jesus gave points to a specific signs and event. He emphasized that He will return immediately after the great tribulation, after the solar eclipse. However, He then promised an adjustment in the time of His coming because of very dangerous conditions that will exist on Earth at that time.

Jesus warned that at that time of His return there will be trouble, and great suffering on Earth. World War-3 will be in progress. Israel will at that time recover from the shocking effects of an invasion by hostile enemies.

The Middle-East war which will trigger a global conflict will most likely take place by 2022. The global war will be catastrophic, and living conditions will be horrifying. Man will be positioned to destroy the Earth with nuclear weapons.

The Lord knows the mind and intention of man, and therefore, will not allow man to destroy the Earth. The Lord will then cut the tribulation period short to save mankind, and to save the planet.

Therefore, it is possible that the Lord could advance the event of the battle of Armageddon as the means of ending World War-3, and also the great tribulation. The battle of Armageddon could well take place at the time of the blood moon of September, 2025. This would fulfill Joel's and John's prediction that the Day of the Lord will take place after the moon turns into blood.

Nonetheless, the solar eclipse of October, 2022 should not be ruled out as the event that relates to the Second Coming. In view of the celestial predictions, and the truth that the time of Christ's return is hidden from the minds of men; it is rather prudent to consider all four eclipses equally qualified as fore-view to the Second Coming.

CHAPTER 27

GLORIOUS RETURN

Scriptures revealed that Jesus will return to Earth at the time after the great tribulation. Jesus also revealed that the Sun will be dark, and the Moon will not give any light. This description of the celestial event indicates that He will return while a solar eclipse is in progress.

The prophet Zechariah affirmed that on the day when the Lord comes, the sunlight will fade away, and the moon and stars will be darkened. The prophet then remarked that the darkness will fade and give place to sunshine in the evening. This strongly suggest that the eclipse of the Sun could be viewed from Jerusalem during the mid-hours of the day.[122]

According to NASA eclipse forecast, there are two solar eclipse events that fits Zechariah's prophecy. One eclipse on Tuesday, October 25, 2022, and the other on August 2, 2027 could be viewed from Jerusalem between the hours of 11:40 AM and 3.22 PM. In both instances, the day will start with sunshine, then it will be darkened, and sunlight will return in the evening.

The entire Middle-East region will be plunged into an eerie darkness. As the scary subtle darkness sets in over Jerusalem, a dramatic burst of light suddenly fills the darkened skies. Then suddenly, a great angelic host dressed in white robes will fill the skies.

The heavens will open, and the sign of the Son of Man will appear in the sky. Jesus Christ will appear in all His majestic glory, shining like the Sun. He will be dressed in splendor and grandeur, and will appear riding a white horse. The troops of heaven dressed in dazzling white robes, and riding on horses will follow Him.

Following behind will be tens of thousands of His saints who were caught up to Jesus in the rapture. These are the born-again believers, who lived according to the word of God. They are the spirit-filled believers comprising of the true church. The scriptures said that they were redeemed unto God by the blood of Jesus, and came from every tribe, and nation and people on Earth.[123] They will be dressed in white robes, and riding on white horses, in the company of Christ and the armies of heaven.[124]

Christ will return to Earth a victorious king, who defeated the nations in the battle of Armageddon. His title will be King of Kings, and Lord of Lords, and will rule over all the nations of the Earth.

All eyes shall will see Him as He comes to Earth riding on the clouds.[125] People will beat their chests, wail, and mourn in anguish when they see Jesus coming in the clouds. The Lord will come to Jerusalem. His feet will touch down on Mount of Olives from where he ascended 2,000 years earlier.

The rulers of the Earth and their military people will be scared, and will call out to the rocks, and the mountains to fall on them, and hide them from the King of Heaven, and from the vengeance of the Lamb.

There will be no hiding place for the ordinary people, nor for those who destroyed the Earth. The Beast (Antichrist) and the false prophet will be captured. They will be immediately judged and sentenced. The Bible says that the Beast and the false prophet will be thrown alive into the lake of fire.[126]

All the kings and rulers and troops who fought against the Lord in the battle of Armageddon will be captured. Likewise, all the people who had the mark of the Beast, or worshipped or paid homage to the Beast or his statue, or gave him divine honors will be captured, and executed by the sword.

Jesus Christ will enter into Jerusalem as a victorious commander-in-chief. The Jews will acknowledge Him as their Messiah. They will be filled with joy and happiness, and grateful for their deliverance from the ruthless enemies.

Some will observe the scars on His hands, and will ask Him how He came by those wounds. Messiah will answer and say that He received those wounds in the house of His friends. Then, the people will recall to mind the One who was crucified by the Romans 2000 years ago.

The Jews will recall the day their forefathers brought Jesus to Pilate. They will recall the day they shouted at the top of their voices, "crucify Him, Crucify Him." They will recall the day when the Roman soldiers nailed Jesus to the cross. They will visualize Jesus hanging upon the cross, and on the little hill outside the walls of Jerusalem. They will recall looking at Him, naked, bruised, and bloodied. They will visualize blood spewing from His hands and feet, as He writhed, and groaned in pain and agony on the cross.

The Jews will be sorry for the affliction, pain, and the suffering of Jesus at the hand of the heathens, on account of their Jewish forefathers, centuries ago. They will admit the grave misdeed of their forefathers, who through religious piety, and willful ignorance, blindly rejected their unrecognized Messiah, and were complicit in His crucifixion.

The Jews will be filled with remorse. They will mourn with overwhelming sorrow for blindly rejecting their unrecognized Messiah throughout the centuries. The Jews will repent for their transgressions, and there will be a great period of mourning in the land of Israel.

The Lord will show mercy to His people. He will open up a fountain of grace in Jerusalem, and cleanse the Jews of their transgressions, and uncleanliness. From that time on they shall be His people, and they shall recognize Him as their God and Messiah.

CHAPTER 28

A NEW WORLD ORDER

The Common Era began 2,000 years ago with peace and good will at the birth of Jesus. Conversely, the era will end with a bang at the Second Coming of Jesus. There will be a horrific world war, the nations will be angry, and they will employ the deadliest weapons ever invented by man. Nuclear bombs will explode in anger, and there will be destruction and death everywhere.

Then comes the battle of Armageddon, and man will face off with a furious God. There will be torrential rains, terrific flashes of lightning, and dreadful peals of thunder at the onset of the battle. Suddenly, there will be fiery meteors striking the Earth at tremendous speeds. Finally, there will be a tremendously powerful earthquake that will reshape the surface of the Earth in many places.

The world will be filled with terrified and traumatized people. Man has failed to manage the world under the Common Era. Therefore, a change in the social order is inevitable.

After Armageddon, the Earth will experience the dawning of a new era. This era will be called the Kingdom Age. In due time, Christ will return to Earth, and take control of the planet from man. He will immediately set up His throne in Jerusalem, and begin his earthly reign as King of Kings, and Lord of Lords. This era shall last for 1,000 years, and Christ the Messiah shall reign over the Earth for the entire age.

Christ's government will be a theocracy. His servants will be drawn from the resurrected saints, and the redeemed church that was caught up to heaven. God will make them kings and priests, to serve Him in His kingdom during the kingdom age.[127] And those saints shall live and reign with Christ for 1,000 years.[128]

Messiah's kingdom shall be supreme. Christ will be King over all the nations of the world. And the King - the all-powerful Ruler, the Omnipotent God shall shepherd, and control the nations with a rod of iron.[129]

Messiah's kingdom shall be universal. It will be a one world government, and the law and the word of the Lord shall go forth from Jerusalem.

The kingdom will be peaceful. The Messiah will judge among the nations, and reprimand strong nations. A decree shall go forth from Jerusalem to outlaw all international conflicts. The nations will be ordered to destroy their weapons of war, and make them into useful civil tools. There will be no negotiations nor treaty. All nations great and small must promptly comply. The law will come from Jerusalem, and the decree will be final.

All nuclear weapons will be destroyed, likewise all biological and chemical weapons. All tanks, missiles, heavy guns, and all implements of war will be destroyed. Warships, submarines and military aircrafts, and other implements of war will be restructured for civil purposes. Nations shall no more learn war, or practice war games, or fight against one another anymore.[130]

Messiah's kingdom shall be secure, and all people will live in peace and prosperity. They shall walk in the name of the Lord, and seek after righteousness all the days of their lives.

The nations will have one major obligation. They will be required to visit Jerusalem every year in order to celebrate the Feast of the Tabernacles. All nations that refuse to go up to Jerusalem to worship the King, the Lord of Hosts will be severely punished. The Lord will strike those nations with a plague, and no rain shall fall upon their country:[131] Messiah will be the supreme ruler of all the nations, and the Lord will be magnified forever.

REFERENCES

Chapter 1

1   Source: Daniel 8:13-14

2   Source: NASA captures double eclipse of the sun.by John Zuhisdorf, http://www.sott.net/article/301806-NASA-captures-a-double-eclipse-of-the-sun

3   Source: Genesis 1:14

4   Source: Daniel 5:26

5   Source: Genesis 1:14 Amp

Chapter 2

6   Source: Daniel 12:1

7   Source: Revelation 3:10

8   Source: Matthew 24:22

9   Source: Daniel 8:14

10   Source: Daniel 9:27, 11:3, 12:1, Matthew 24:15

11   Source: Revelation 12:10

12   Source: Daniel 8:23

13   Source: Luke 23:18

14   Source: Zephaniah 3:3

15   Source: Jeremiah 30:5-7

16   Source: Daniel 7:25, Revelation 3:10, 6:8, 13:7

17   Source: Revelation 13:15-16

18   Source: Daniel 9:26-27

Chapter 3

19	Source: Malachi 4:5, Revelation 11:3	
20	Source: Malachi 4:5	
21	Source: Jude 14	
22	Source: Genesis 5:22	
23	Source: Malachi 4:5-6	
24	Source: Gospel of Nicodemus 20:3-4	
25	Source: Gospel of Nicodemus 20:3	
26	Source: Malachi 4:5-6	

Chapter 4

27	Source: Daniel 11:36
28	Source: Daniel 8:23
29	Source: Daniel 8:24, Revelation 13:2
30	Source: Matthew 4:8-9
31	Source: 2 Thessalonians 2:11
32	Source: Daniel 8:12

Chapter 5

33	Source: Daniel 7:8, 21, Revelation 13:5,7
34	Source: Revelation 13: 8
35	Source: 2 Thessalonians 2:4, Daniel 11:36-37, Ezekiel 28:2
36	Source: Revelation 13:8
37	Source: Revelation 13:5
38	Source: Daniel 8:11-13
39	Source: Daniel 7:25, Revelation 13:7
40	Source: Daniel 8:13
41	Source: Revelation 13:3

42	Source: Daniel 3:5, Revelation 3:10 & 13:15	

Chapter 6

43	Source: Revelation 3:10 & 6:9,11 & 20:4	
44	Source: Revelation 6:9, 11	

Chapter 7

45	Source: Revelation 17:11	
46	Source: Daniel 5:21b	
47	Source: Proverbs 21:1	
48	Source: Isaiah 44:28, 45:1	
49	Source: Jeremiah 25:11-12	
50	Source: Matthew 7:22-23	
51	Source: Nahum 1:3	
52	Source: Daniel 9:25	
53	Source: Daniel 4:35, 5:21	

Chapter 9

54	Source: Daniel 4:25	
55	Source: Jeremiah 25:11	
56	Source: Jeremiah 25:12	
57	Source: Isaiah 2:2, Micah 4:1 (NIV)	
58	Source: Isaiah 2:2, Micah 4:1	

Chapter 11

59	Source: Luke 21:25	
60	Source: Joel 2:31	
61	Source: Matthew 24:6	
62	Source: Matthew 24:7	

63	Source: Matthew 19:4-5
64	Source: Leviticus 20:13
65	Source: Matthew 24:15

Chapter 12

66	Source: 2nd Samuel 24:15
67	Source: 2nd Samuel 24:13, 15
68	Source: Psalm 8:5-6, Hebrews 2:7 Genesis 1:28
69	Source: Ecclesiastes 12:13 AMP
70	Source: Psalm 115:16 AMP
71	Source: Daniel 4:35 Amp
72	Source: Ezekiel 38:22,23 Amp

Chapter 13

| 73 | Source: Revelation 6:1-17 |

Chapter 14

74	Source: Galatians 5:22-23
75	Source: Revelation 6: 11 AMP
76	Source: Revelation 11:18 NIV
77	Source: Revelation 7:14
78	Source: Matthew 24:27

Chapter 16

| 79 | Source: Daniel 8:14 |
| 80 | Source: John 14:2-3 |

Chapter 17

| 81 | Source: Matthew 24:29-31 |
| 82 | Source: 1st Thessalonians *4:15-17* |

Chapter 18

    83   Source: Ezekiel 38:2-8, 14

Chapter 19

    84   Source: Zechariah 14:2

Chapter 20

    85   Source: Zechariah 14:2

    86   Source: Joel 2:2

    87   Source: Daniel 12:1

    88   Source: Jeremiah 30:7

    89   Source: Matthew 24:21

    90   Source: Matthew 24:21

    91   Source: Zechariah 13:8

    92   Source: Zechariah 14:2

Chapter 21

    93   Source: Luke 21:24

    94   Source: Daniel 8: 11-13

    95   Source: Daniel 12:11

    96   Source: Malachi 4:5-6

    97   Source: Zechariah 14:2

    98   Source: Zechariah 13:90

    99   Source: Ezekiel 38:18

Chapter 22

    100   Source: Matthew 24:22

Chapter 23

    101   Source: Revelation 11:18

102   Source: Revelation 11:15

103   Source: Genesis 1:28, 2:15

104   Source: Genesis 9:6

105   Source: Luke 21:24

Chapter 24

106   Source: Revelation *11:15*

Chapter 25

107   Source: Zechariah 12:9

108   Source: Joel 3:2

109   Source: Revelation 16:17

110   Source: Zachariah 14:4

111   Source: Zechariah 14: 8, 10

112   Source: Revelation 16:18-20

Chapter 26

113   Source: Luke 21:27

114   Source: Acts 1:11

115   Source: Revelation 1:7

116   Source: Daniel 8:14

117   Source: Matthew 24:29

118   Source: Joel 2:31

119   Source: Revelation 6:12

120   Source: Matthew 24:29

121   Source: Fred Espenak, NASA

Chapter 27

122   Source: Zechariah 14:5-7

123   Source: Revelation 5:9

124   Source: Revelation 19:14

125   Source: Revelation 1:7

126   Source: Revelation 19:20

Chapter 28

127   Source: Revelation 1: 6, 5:10

128   Source: Revelation 20:4

129   Source: Revelation 12:5 & 19:15

130   Source: Micah 4:3

131   Source: Zechariah 14:16-17

www.ingramcontent.com/pod-product-compliance
Lightning Source LLC
LaVergne TN
LVHW051601080426
835510LV00020B/3076